LIFE
IS A
MOUNTAIN

GOD'S FAITHFULNESS IN THE LIFE OF DONALD NORBIE

Donald Norbie

Life is a Mountain

God's Faithfulness in the Life of Donald Norbie

LIFE IS A MOUNTAIN
GOD'S FAITHFULNESS
IN THE LIFE OF DONALD NORBIE
By: Donald L. Norbie
Copyright © 2009
GOSPEL FOLIO PRESS
All Rights Reserved

Published by
GOSPEL FOLIO PRESS
304 Killaly St. W.
Port Colborne, ON L3K 6A6
CANADA

ISBN: 9781897117934

Cover design by Rachel Brooks
Cover Photo: The peaks of the Garden of the Gods
against snow covered Pikes Peak.

All Scripture quotations from the
King James Version unless otherwise noted.

Printed in USA

Contents

In Appreciation 7
The Life Of Donald L. Norbie 9
1. The Early Years 11
2. Arizona Bound! 17
3. Tucson and the Desert 21
4. Navy Days 31
   Decaying Hopes 45
5. A Carrier and a Destroyer 49
6. College Years At Westmont 57
7. A Busy Year At Wheaton 65
8. Emmaus Bible School 75
9. Oklahoma, the Sooner State 87
10. A New Assembly 97
11. A New House & Bible Camp 109
12. A Difficult Decision 121
13. Colorado Bound 137
14. A Death and Rebirth 147

Appendix
    Life Is A Mountain 157
        A Challange 161
    In Journeys Often 165
    Workers' and Elders' Conferences 175
    Koinonia house history 179
    Epilogue 182

In Appreciation

I would like to dedicate this account of our lives together to my wife of nearly sixty years, Edna Marie Adams Norbie. We met in college and married June 7, 1947 in San Gabriel, California. Through the years she has been a faithful, devoted wife to me. I trusted her with everything.

Marie, as I called her, had a Swedish mother whose parents emigrated from Sweden and settled near Albin, Wyoming, where they developed a homestead.

Her father came from old American stock, with English predominating, and grew up in Illinois on a farm. Marie graduated from college in 1946 and taught school for one year before we married.

We worked for a wealthy family the first year of our marriage while I finished college. She was the maid and I was the handy man. There she learned to entertain beautifully and this became a special ministry of her life. Many have eaten at our table and enjoyed her tasty cooking.

Among our early guests was Jim Elliott, later killed in Ecuador, a dear friend. She could have worked outside of the home but instead devoted herself to her family. Marie was a hard worker and made our house an attractive home. She was good at economizing, canning and freezing produce from our garden, sewing and mending clothes.

She has loved the Lord and has been a good Bible student, teaching many children and adult women. Marie has been the first to edit my writing, profiting from her journalism classes in school. In my serving the Lord I have been gone at times and she never complained over my absence but maintained the household faithfully. During lean times financially I never heard her complain nor wish for a different life. My life has been so intertwined with hers that I would find it very difficult to live without her. I could wish to go home before she does. I thank God for such a faithful, loving wife.

LIFE IS A MOUNTAIN

"Her children rise up and call her blessed; Her husband also, and he praises her. Many daughters have done well, But you excel them all" (Prov. 31:28-29).

Donald L. Norbie
November 30, 2006

The Life Of Donald L. Norbie

As the years pass and life is winding down, it is natural to reminisce and to review one's life for succeeding generations. Three of my grandparents died while I was young and I know very little about them. At a family reunion, some of my cousins were asking about my mother's father, they had never met him. Because I had lived with him for some months they asked me, "What was he like?" This book is written for our children and grandchildren and perhaps may be a blessing to others. It is my desire to glorify the Lord, to show how He saved a teenage boy and faithfully preserved him through all the varied experiences of life. God is faithful!

My prayer is that the reading of this account may be used by God to draw some to the Saviour in salvation, and then to encourage them to become true disciples of the Lord Jesus. There is no better life than that of a disciple of the Lord Jesus and it brings eternal reward. Paul encouraged Timothy to a life of godliness, *"For bodily exercise profits a little, but godliness is profitable for all things, having promise of the life that now is and of that which is to come"* (1 Tim. 4:8). My regret is that I have only one life to live for my Lord. May God give grace to finish life well.

> From prayer that asks that I may be
> Sheltered from winds that beat on Thee,
> From fearing when I should aspire,
> From faltering when I should climb higher,
> From silken self, O Captain, free
> Thy soldier who would follow Thee.
> ~Amy Carmichael~

Donald Norbie
March 27, 2002

1

THE EARLY YEARS

It was a beautiful fall day in Willmar, Minnesota as Nels Norbie walked excitedly down the street handing out cigars to all who came by. He kept repeating over and over, "It's a boy; it's a boy!" His first born was a son and they named him Donald LeRoy. The birth took place in the office of Dr. Frost across from the hotel.

Nels' parents sailed from Stavanger, Norway to the United States, met and married in Iowa. Their names were Rasmus (b. 1874) and Tillie Nelson Warburg (b. 1876), good Norwegian names! They had immigrated from Stavanger, where they had lived on small, picturesque islands in the bay.

Like many others they were hoping for a better life in the States, where rich farm land was plentiful and cheap. Nels was born in Iowa, one of eight children. There were four boys and four girls. The family soon moved to Minnesota where Rasmus farmed the rest of his life in the Willmar area.

Like many of that era Nels graduated from the eighth grade and then went to work. He worked as a farm hand for neighboring farmers and later went to work for the railroad on the section crew. It was hard work with meager wages but he was young and strong. Like most Scandinavians Nels' parents were Lutherans. As a baby he was baptized in a Norwegian church, Green Lake Lutheran Church, and was later confirmed. Church was a vital, social part of community life but strong, personal faith was more rare All had been baptized, were church members and assumed they were Christians.

In his late teens Nels met a young girl named Myrtle Viola Carlson, who also had lived on a farm in that area. A little lake on their farm was named Carlson Lake and brought much enjoyment to the children growing up.

Her parents were John Edward Carlson, often called Eddie (b. 1872), and Caroline Dengerud (b. 1879). Caroline's father, Ole T. Dengerud, had come from Norway in 1865 and Eddie's parents had come from Sweden. The first language for the children was Norwegian but the children soon learned to speak English. They were second generation and were Americans in culture.

Viola, as she was called, and Nels fell in love and were married in 1922. They were young and strong, full of dreams for the future. Nels worked for the railroad at first and later worked for a small store in Spicer, a picturesque village on Green Lake, a beautiful, large lake with crystal clear water. In time he became a partner and the store was named Banker & Norbie: Groceries, Dry goods and Farm Produce. Later he took over the store from Mr. Banker. It looked like a good future for Nels and he was enjoying life with his wife and son Donald.

Viola became pregnant again and they were both excited about the possibility of another child. But she became sickly that winter and the doctor became very concerned. She could not seem to regain her strength and coughed a lot. Tests were run and one day in February the doctor came to Nels' store, and pulled him aside. He said, "Nels, I am sorry. I have bad news for you. Viola has T. B." T. B.! My father said that he wept like a baby. His wife had tuberculosis, a killer disease in those days and she was pregnant with his second child.

There were no drugs for T. B. at that time. All a doctor could do was to prescribe rest and hope for some healing. But Viola was not doing at all well and the decision was made to send her to a sanatorium. May 7, 1927 Viola was sent to Riverside Sanatorium in Granite Falls and our happy, little family was broken up. The decision was made to send Donald to live with Grandpa Carlson in Willmar. Grandma Carlson had died in 1921 before Nels and Viola had married but two younger sisters were still at home and they would care for Donald. Marvel and Helen were very loving and kind to a little, homesick boy, who often went to sleep crying. But there were happy times too. My Uncle Roy still lived at home and drove an oil truck, delivering fuel for Mobil Oil. At times I would ride with him as he delivered fuel to the farmers. He was a favorite uncle of mine and called me Donny to his dying day.

My father took me down occasionally to see mother. The sanatorium grounds were like a park, lush and green, shaded by majestic, tall trees, bordered by the tranquil waters of the Minnesota River. I was overjoyed to see my mother again but there would be tearful partings when it was time to go home. I longed to feel my mother's arms around me, but I learned to stay at arm's length. T. B. was fearfully infectious. It had started in the family, taking my grandmother. Now my mother had this dread disease and her sister, Victoria, also had it and would die in a few years. No doubt my father wondered, "Who will be next?"

Viola went into labor and delivered a healthy little boy on September 25, 1927. Because of her infectious disease the doctor took the baby immediately from the room. Her mother's heart must have longed to hold him and to love him but it would be years before she would even be able to touch him. Grandma Norbie took him home, loved him and raised him as one of her own. She had never learned English well and Norwegian was spoken in the home. Kenneth learned to speak Norwegian with a Stavanger accent! I was told I had a brother but was not raised with him, something we both regret to this day.

Then my life changed again. My Grandpa Ed became deathly ill and died April 9, 1929. It was my first real experience with death. There was much weeping and sorrow filled the rooms of the house. The body was laid in state in the living room. Family and friends entered the house quietly and reverently, viewing the body and consoling the family. I remember standing before the casket, filled with awe and wonder—and foreboding.

My grandfather who had taken me in, loved me and given me a safe place was dead. He lay there, cold and unresponsive, and I was filled with fear. No longer would he play with me. I was only five and I discovered that death was a robber and a fearful enemy. What would happen to me now?

A picture taken when I was about a year old shows a happy, exuberant baby. Later a picture was taken of the two brothers; Kenneth was about one year old and I was five. Kenneth is bubbling and happy but I sit quietly with a pensive air. The sorrows of life weighed heavily upon a young boy's heart.

It was decided that I should go to live at the Norbie's farm. The future of our family was very uncertain. How long would mother be in the sanatorium? Farm life was very different from the town. I liked the animals and there were always chores to be done. Grandma was also raising my cousin Luverne, who was two years younger than me. We became good friends then and are to this day. I remember helping with potato harvest, going through the fields after they were dug, picking them up and sacking them. But it turned out that my time on the farm would be brief.

In the fall it was decided that Viola could come home; her disease was in an arrested state. September 27 she came home and the three of us were together again. Because of her weakened condition it was decided Kenneth would stay with the grandparents. Dad had rented a comfortable house across the road from Green Lake. I loved that lake; it was perhaps ten miles across and to a little boy it was like an ocean. His business was going well in Spicer and it was time for me to start school. School was about a mile away, just a nice walk. And mother was home.

The fall was beautiful with the leaves bursting with color before losing their grip and drifting slowly to the ground. I was enjoying school and so thankful to be at home with my parents. But then winter came, a long, cold Minnesota winter. I could enjoy the snow and winter sports. There was the excitement too of watching men from the Great Northern Railroad cutting and storing ice for summer use in the refrigerated cars. But winter was hard on mother. She was down in bed most of the time When spring and summer came she improved again and our hopes revived. Maybe she would get well. During these years she did much handcraft; hooked and braided rugs, embroidered pictures and beaded flowers. She took a first place in the Minnesota State Fair with her beaded flowers in 1929. Her fingers were always busy.

My dad raised rabbits that year and I liked to play around the hutches. One day the mailman came to the door and told my father he wanted to buy a rabbit. My father went with him to choose one. He pointed to me in one of the cages where I was playing and said, "I'll take that one!"

Fall came again and another hard winter. Mother had a bad time. Her T. B. was active again. The doctor was concerned. He said, "Nels, you may lose Viola if you stay here. These cold winters will kill her. She may heal and do well if you get to a dry, warm climate like Arizona." It was a big decision to make. He would have to give up his business and a depression made jobs scarce. It would mean leaving all of our family behind and Arizona seemed as far away as Timbuktu. What should we do?.

Enroute to Nels' Work camp

Donald and Kenneth 1927

THE EARLY YEARS

Nels and Viola (My Parents) 1922

Nels Norbie
Family and his parents 1937

LIFE IS A MOUNTAIN

Trip to Arizona 1931

2
Arizona Bound!

Finally during the spring of 1931 the decision was made. We would move to Arizona. These were depression years and my father had a good business. It was hard to give it up and sell the buisness. We would have to leave family behind, all of our relatives, including my brother Kenneth. But to stay would mean the likely death of Mother. It was one of life's hard choices. The business had to be sold. Nels had been an agent for Litchfield Produce, buying eggs, poultry, cream and hides for them. They wrote a favourable letter, commending him for being industrious, honest, and thoroughly capable. But what kind of work could he get in Arizona during depression days?

Nels bought a four wheel trailer and we began to sort through things, deciding what we would take and what we would sell. Furniture and larger items had to be sold. My father loved to hunt and fish so we would take along a tent and camping equipment. We had a 1929 Ford Model A to pull the trailer. It was a two-door and the passenger seat could fold back to make a bed for Mother. An auction was held on June 2, 1931, which brought in $377.55. Family gifts, from a family reunion before we left, amounted to $66.20. There were tearful goodbyes and we wondered if we would ever see these loved ones again. Arizona seemed so remote. We had to say goodbye to beautiful Green Lake and to the lush fields and trees of Minnesota. We were bound for the desert.

LIFE IS A MOUNTAIN

We left Spicer on June 3, bound for Arizona, pulling our trailer, looking like Gypsies! We camped along the way and it was a long, hard trip. Our route took us down into Texas and then to El Paso, across New Mexico and southern Arizona to Yuma, arriving in Yuma on June 11. I believe my father had some contact in Yuma. We rented a small house and Dad went to work in a shed where they were shipping out melons. We could buy melons for a penny a piece! There were many irrigated fields around Yuma, watered by the Colorado River. It was hot, fearfully hot, and there was no air conditioning. Because we had come from cool Minnesota, to the searing, desert heat was more than we could take. It would be 100 degrees at night and much hotter during the day. My sick mother was suffering. Dad heard of Prescott, a mile high and cool with a mild climate. It was decided we would move up there and look around for a place to settle.

We left Yuma on June 22 and headed for Prescott. There is a steep grade going up to Prescott and a hot, desert, tail wind was blowing. Cars would overheat, and have to pull off the road. Trucks drove up and down the road, selling water. It was a slow trip but the Model A made it, pulling a heavily loaded trailer. That was a tough little car.

We looked around Prescott and then Dad decided to look at Oak Creek Canyon. We were told it was a beautiful area. We drove to Jerome and then down that wild grade with the trailer pushing us. But after looking around the area, Prescott looked quite good and we came back up the steep grade through Jerome. It was a tough, old, mining town, with houses clinging to the steep mountainside in desperation, struggling to keep from sliding down into the valley below.

That summer we camped under the pines on the side of a mountain on the outskirts of Prescott. We cooked with a camp stove and lived very simply. My mother was a very patient person; she never complained. Work was scarce but my father was a hard worker and was willing to do anything. He worked for some time, cutting timber for a dollar a day. Later he got a job at the Salvation Army, helping with the distribution of food and clothing to the needy. They had a model T truck that he drove to pick up items.

We needed a house in which to live. One day we heard that a couple was going back to Arkansas and they wanted to sell their place. It was a small house, only one large room; they had plans to build a large house in front later. There was no electricity or running water. An outhouse sat at the back. But there were several lots, maybe an acre, and it was located near the forest and mountains.

We could have animals and a garden. We decided to buy it. As I recall, it cost around $500.00 and we were able to pay cash for it with some money from Mother's inheritance. We had a home, the first one my parents owned. They had rented in Minnesota.

The water came from a dug well with a wooden cover. A windlass with a bucket, pulled the water up. It was sweet, cold water. One year the well went dry and had to be dug deeper. I remember pulling the dirt up in a bucket. Life was simple with a wood stove for both cooking and heating. A kerosene lamp gave light after dark. Although we were poor we always had enough food and I loved it there. We had animals: goats for milk, chickens, pigeons and dogs. One of our dogs was a little Boston terrier named Tiny. The other, a beautiful German Shepherd, had been given to us. His coat was silver tipped and I named him Frosty. I wanted a horse, too, but Dad said we could not afford to feed one. It was a great place for a boy to play cowboys and Indians, letting my imagination run free. Prescott winters are mild we could play outside year round.

I began school that fall at Miller Valley School, about a mile away. I became a voracious reader and soon read all the books in the school library. Then I would go to the City Library. Prescott was a small, mining and ranching town of several thousand people, but it did have a library. There was a boy at school who was a little larger than I was and he was a bully. He began to chase me home from school, threatening to beat me up. One day I had enough of that. I said to him, "I'll fight you after school." So after school there was a cluster of boys gathered around the two of us and we went at it. It was short. I bloodied his nose and he knocked a little chip out of one of my teeth. We both decided to call it quits and he never bothered me again. I decided there is a time when you have to fight.

I began to collect arrow heads and other Indian relics. One day I noticed a neighbor was using a beautiful tomahawk head for a door stop. I thought, "That man does not even appreciate it; I could use it in my collection." When no one was looking I took it and slipped it into my box with my arrow heads. One day my dad was looking over the collection and asked me where I got it. I could not lie to him and told him the truth. My conscience convicted me; I was a thief. He said, "You take it back!" As I took it back I began to realize that I was a sinner, I was not right with God.

My father got a job at the Arizona Pioneers' Home, a retirement facility for the elderly. He worked in the kitchen and dining room. A picture of him along with the staff and all the 170 residents appeared in a Phoenix paper, April 11, 1934. These were real pioneers, some dating back to the Civil War. He kept a paper with the names of many who had given him a Christmas gift. Most gave him 25 cents, although one gave him a whole dollar! Anyway, it showed appreciation of his help.

March 2, 1935, he handed in his resignation and received a letter of commendation. As I recall he had some altercation with one of the supervisors and decided to leave. My father did have a temper at times and may have lost it on that occasion. Anyway the decision was made to move. It was traumatic for me for I loved our home, our animals and the mountains. But I was not consulted!

It was decided that we would move to Tucson. The doctors thought that a little warmer climate would benefit my mother's health. She still was not doing well. Tucson was at about 2,200 feet and was warmer than Prescott but not as hot as Yuma. We had built on to the house and were able to rent it. The day we sold all our animals was a sad day for me. All our belongings were once again loaded into that trailer and we headed for Tucson. It was March, 1935, during the heart of the Depression.

3

Tucson and the Desert

Tucson rarely sees snow and the winters are very mild, which was good for mother's health. It is a greener desert than Yuma, with lots of creosote bushes and all kinds of cacti. There are some mesquite and palo verde trees. Rainfall is sparse, about eight inches a year. Tucson is in a large valley surrounded by mountains at some distance. I keenly missed the pines and mountains of Prescott, though.

We located a small, three room house for rent in Duke's Court on S. 8th Avenue, near the Veteran's Hospital. Mr. Duke had a number of small houses for rent for $10.00 a month. Our house was linked to the next house by a double garage with a bathroom at the back which we shared with the neighboring house. There was a shower but no hot water. We also had water in the house, a small wood stove for heat in the winter and a kerosene stove for cooking. It was quite spartan but it became my home for the next seven years. Since there was no insulation it became fearfully hot in the summer. The house had three rooms: a very small kitchen, a small bedroom in which I slept and a living room where mother's bed was.

Dad had various jobs for several months—anything to put food on the table. Then on October 7th he was able to get a regular job, working for the Dept. of Agriculture. The men worked up in the mountains exterminating wild cotton, which was a host for the boll weevil. He made $44.00 a month. It was hard work, clambering up and down mountain sides, pulling up the wild cotton by hand. In December they saw he had some leadership ability and made him a foreman with a crew of twenty men. This was a help financially; he now made $66.00 a month.

Dad was usually gone from Monday to Friday working in the mountains where they had a camp for the men. They had to walk in for some miles and used donkeys to pack in supplies. One week he arranged for me to come up for a few days. Their camp was high in the Santa Catalina Mountains among the pines. I rode in on a donkey named Chongo, a memorable trip for a young boy. The men killed lots of rattle snakes while working. Dad would bring them home, skin them and sell the skins, which were popular for purses and belts. We did what we could to make a little extra money. One time he brought home a little coyote, which we kept for a while but then gave to a local zoo.

Because we moved in the middle of a semester I was sent back a half grade in school, which I made up later in summer school. Moving is hard on children. One has to adjust to a new teacher and make other friends. After I finished grade school, I went to Safford Jr. High and had to ride the school bus. It was a school with many Mexican Americans, some of whom became my friends. I do not remember any racial bias there.

With a better salary my father decided we could afford a newer car. So in the summer of 1936 we traded in our faithful Model A for a 1936 Ford V8. My dad kept the registration card on it, dated August 26. It was a demonstrator so it was discounted; I believe it cost around $500.00. That was our pride and joy and my father kept it for many years, until well after the war. With a better car it was decided we could finally make a trip back to Minnesota.

We set off August 14, 1937, for the lush green of Minnesota. There was a drought, but still it was green compared to Tucson. It took several days and Mother lay down on the back seat much of the way. She still was not strong and tired quickly. I wondered if she would ever get well. We always scalded the dishes after eating and were very health conscious. I knew I lived with a killer disease. It had taken my grandmother and one of my aunts.

Our time in Minnesota was a happy time of family reunions; we had not seen family for six years. There were picnics with the Carlsons, Mother's side of the family, and good times with the Norbies too. It was great to see my Grandma and Grandpa Norbie again. There was some discussion of possibly taking Kenneth back with us, but it was decided against. Mother's health was too precarious and Kenneth was really at home with his grandparents. When the time came to leave, there were tearful good-byes, and we set off again for Arizona. We had a safe trip home and I was soon back in school.

We had a radio now and mother began listening to various Bible teaching programs. Her heart opened to the Lord and she accepted Him as her Lord and Saviour. Now she began to read the Bible hungrily and to grow spiritually. One of the programs to which she listened was conducted by T. B. Gilbert, a local preacher who had moved from Indiana for his wife's health. Mother wrote him of her interest and he began to visit our home. One day he visited after school when I was home. Before he left he prayed and I was deeply moved. I was used to saying prayers but this man prayed as if he knew God. When he finished, he saw my tears and asked me, "Would you like to be saved?" I knew I was a sinner and was not right with God. He went over God's plan of salvation and told me that Christ's death on the cross was enough to pay for my sins. That afternoon with tears I received the Lord Jesus as my Lord and Saviour. He left me with John 5:24 and told me to cling to God's promise. It was March 2, 1938, the most momentous day of my life.

Little did I know what a furor this would cause in our family. While living in Prescott we had not gone to church because there was no Lutheran Church in our area. When we moved to Tucson, we, that is my father and I, began attending a Lutheran Church. Mother still was not well enough to go. We went to church for one hour on Sunday and it was a formal routine. I do not remember any of the messages. All of us were baptized and presumed to be Christians. But I did not mind going because I was learning to drive the car on the way to church! My father became very upset when I told him I was now saved. He said,

"You have always been a Christian; we had you baptized." He decided to have the Lutheran preacher talk to me to straighten me out. The preacher assured me that I had always been a Christian and not to get confused by any religious experiences. I felt frustrated; he did not understand what salvation was. I realized that he had not given me the gospel and now wanted to talk me out of my conversion.

I told my father, "I do not want to go back to that church." He was angry and frustrated, feeling betrayed and deserted. Now he would have to go to church by himself. Mr. Gilbert had been evangelizing and teaching in the area and some had been saved. A few months before my conversion they began to meet as a simple New Testament assembly. I decided I wanted to go there to get teaching, and my mother was supportive. She was delighted that I had turned to the Lord. I had been very rebellious against my parents before, defying her when my father was gone, and now God was working in my life. An older Christian, Mr. Livingston, would come by in his Model A and take me to the meetings.

The fellowship rented the Demolay Hall for Sunday meetings. The Wednesday prayer meeting was held in homes. Dances would be held on Saturday nights in the hall. The assembly would come in Sunday morning and put the chairs in order. It was a small group for the Lord's Supper, the chairs were arranged in a circle around the table. On my first visit I sat quietly in wonder, waiting to see what was going to happen. Some brothers gave out hymns; some read Scriptures. Others prayed, moving prayers of worship and praise. I remember seeing tears in the eyes of one brother. Then the emblems were passed and we took the bread and the wine. I was greatly moved by the love of God for me. It was a far cry from the formal ritual I had known before, and I loved it. This was now my spiritual family. Mr. Gilbert helped with the assembly, but others, too, were encouraged to use their gifts. It was all delightfully simple.

I was given a Bible and began to read it. It fed my spiritual life. I read about baptism and decided I wanted to be baptized. My father was very opposed to this so Mr. Gilbert urged me to wait, rather than to antagonize him further. I prayed for my father and wanted to be a good son. After about a year he realized that I was not going to change and gave me permission to be baptized. The Christians rented a church building for the occasion and it was a joyous time. As I recall, several were baptized. I rejoiced to obey the Lord and to proclaim my faith. My father would not come and my mother was unable to do so. But she rejoiced and always encouraged me spiritually.

In November of 1938 my grandfather died and my father made a hurried trip back to Minnesota for the funeral. Now both of my grandfathers were gone.

The assembly (local congregation) was active in proclaiming the gospel. Mr. Gilbert loved to preach the gospel and our Sunday night meeting was often given over to evangelism. He also conducted a series of tent meetings in the city one year. One of the brothers had a P.A. system that he would mount on his car and we would have street meetings in the library park. At times I would give my testimony, a little fearful that some one from high school would recognize me! We would cover the park with tracts, desiring to share our faith with others. I helped organize a tract "band" of a few young people and we distributed tracts through various neighborhoods. Sometimes after the night meeting when I was at home there came a growing conviction that God was calling me. It seemed I could hear the Lord saying to me, "Don, I want you to preach and to teach My Word."

I was now in Tucson High School among a student body of about 2,000. I enjoyed school and did quite well, taking a college prep course. Both of my parents wanted me to have an education, something they lacked. A bus, across from the Veterans' Hospital, stopped to pick up students. A friend who lived next door played the trombone and urged me to join the band. In October of 1937 my dad rented a trombone for me from the school and I was in the marching band. One event stands out. We marched in a local parade and our picture appeared in the local newspaper. To my chagrin I was the only one out of step! I only stayed in the band for about a year.

I also took some shop courses that were interesting and

easy. Part of the time I was enrolled in ROTC—I enjoyed the order and discipline of the military. I did not have the time to go out for sports. I had a paper route after school and also had things to do around home. Mother could help some with the cooking but there was much that she could not do. The paper route was a good experience. I could buy my own clothes and save some money. In time I was able to buy a camera after a teacher at school encouraged me in photography. It has been my hobby through the years. My paper route was in a poor section of town and I learned to collect on Friday night, right after payday. Otherwise the money would be spent. The men felt it was their manly right to get drunk and to party on Saturday night.

The next spring we were surprised to have a neighbor bring some mail over for my father. Then Dad confessed to us. He had been corresponding with people in Minnesota about work and was determined to move back. He was tired of our intense interest in the Bible and felt if we could move back to Minnesota we would forget this fanatical religion, this cult. It was a jolt for us. Mother talked to her doctor about the move and he strongly warned against it. She was struggling in Arizona and would never stand a Minnesota winter.

Dad quit his job that summer and prepared to leave. I watched with a heavy heart as he packed his guns and personal effects in our Ford. He said goodbye, kissed us, climbed into the car and set out for Minnesota. I still remember the sinking feeling in my heart as he left. Would he ever come back? Would I see him again? My mother was quite controlled but she wept. I can imagine her pain and sense of abandonment. They had taken their marriage vows together, solemn vows of perpetual faithfulness. She never saw him again. It was a black day, Friday, July 7, 1939.

Now I was the man of the house. I had a bike and my paper route. For years I had helped with some of the house work. Now I also had the laundry to do on Saturday, using a wash tub and scrub board. The shopping also fell to me. Mother would make up a shopping list and I would ride my bike about two miles to the Chinese market. We usually spent about $3.50 for groceries on Saturday and the store would deliver the order to our door. A chuck roast would last us all week. We had a refrigerator now; what a luxury in Arizona heat! Dad had bought it a few years earlier. Before that we had used an evaporative water cooler for our food.

Father did not support us and mother applied for help from the State. They offered to help us with $35.00 a month. Mother put aside $3.50 of that for the Lord's work, a powerful example for me in my life. For her, God always had to come first. We adjusted to life, the two of us. The Lord was precious to us and the fellowship of the believers was supportive. We read and prayed together. My mother never spoke ill of my father and never complained. She was a radiant Christian, full of faith; Romans 8:28 was a favorite verse. Mother was a good manager of our meager funds. Ten dollars went for rent, and because my father had left us, Mr. Duke never raised the rent. There was a small electric bill and then the food bill. We ate healthfully but frugally! I would make my lunch and take it to school on the bus. As the months went by, we reluctantly became accepting of the fact that my father was not coming back.

Our doctor was Dr. Watson, who himself had recovered from T.B. in Tucson. He was a compassionate, kind man and never charged us for his visits. His chauffeur would drive him up to our house in his luxurious Packard and park in front of our humble home. He visited Mother regularly and was a great encouragement, ministering to her physical needs. We witnessed to him; I hope I shall see him in heaven. When I married, he sent a wedding gift, always thoughtful and generous.

The years were passing and we never heard from my father. Then finally a legal document arrived, a notice that divorce proceedings were underway. My mother chose not to contest it and the divorce was finalized on July 14, 1941. She was charged with wilful desertion! A six months waiting period was required before another marriage could take place. My dear mother quietly wept and continued to pray for him. The excitement and hopes that she had on her wedding day for a wonderful marriage had become ashes in her heart. But God was with her and she would trust Him. She was given the custody of me and Dad took Kenneth. He left the house in

Prescott, which we had been renting, to her. She put it up for sale and sold it for $900.00! I felt sad about that; it was the only home we ever owned as I was growing up.

I graduated from high school that year and wondered what the future would hold. Should I try to go to college? In view of our financial situation, should I even consider such an option? A singing team from Bob Jones College in Cleveland, Tennessee, came through and had a meeting at the First Baptist Church. I went along with a Christian friend, Charles Courtney, who had also just graduated. We both became excited about the prospect of going to a Christian college. My mother said she could manage with the help of neighbors and wanted me to go. A friend offered to help me financially. I applied, was accepted and caught a ride back to Tennessee with Clyde Narramore, who was a teacher at the college. He later became a prominent psychologist.

It was my first exposure to the South, a very different culture from the casual atmosphere of the Southwest. Charles and I shared a room with two other students. Cliff Barrows, who later joined Billy Graham's team, was one of the students that I met. But I soon realized that my mother really needed me at home and I began to pray about what I should do. I worked in the dining hall for 25 cents an hour and tried to be friendly with the kitchen employees. I was warned not to fraternize with the black help; this was the South! All the strict rules of the school troubled me. The upshot was that I withdrew from school and rode the bus back to Tucson, feeling depressed about the whole experience. Mother was delighted to have me home again.

I worked some and prayed about entering the University of Arizona. It was good to be back in the assembly. Then December 7 came and Pearl Harbor! Japan had attacked us and much of our fleet was sunk. We were at war and it was going to be a bloody time. Some friends enlisted; some were drafted. What should I do? After prayer, Mother and I decided I should enter the University for the time being. Classes went well, except for chemistry. I had no high school chemistry and was lost at first, failing the course, but I caught on finally and finished with a passing grade. I took ROTC with a cavalry unit, thinking that if

I went into the service I could go as an officer.

That spring Mother began complaining of back pain. One day when I want giving her a back rub I noticed two vertebra seemed to be protruding. We showed this to Dr. Watson and he became very concerned and had X-rays taken. He came to us with the heartbreaking news that Mother now had T.B. in her spine and must be hospitalized. She would have to lie flat on a bed for months and hope for healing. It was a crushing blow. The decision was made for her to go to the County Hospital and we would give up our house. We rented a garage to store some of our things and sold the rest. We took my dear mother to the hospital. A young Christian family in the assembly, Kermit and Martha Oestrich, invited me to live with them temporarily and let me have a room. I was able to finish out that semester at the University. What should I do now? The war was on and I felt homeless and adrift. How I needed the Lord to give me wisdom.

That summer 1942 I made a trip back to Minnesota to see family once again. I was determined to see Dad again. I got off the bus in Duluth, where he was living, and found my way to his street address, wondering what I would say when I saw him. I knocked on the door expectantly. I still had hopes he would come back to Mother. To my surprise a woman answered the door. I thought I must have the wrong address and asked, "Does Mr. Norbie live here?" The woman said, "Yes, I am Mrs. Norbie. You must be Donald." She invited me in and told me they had been married since August 26, 1941. I was devastated and confused. When dad came home from work he was very affectionate and warm. They showed me a room where I could stay. That evening I went for a long walk up and down the steep hills of Duluth, tears running down my face and crying out to God. I decided I would have to accept the reality of his marriage and try to have a relationship with his wife and her daughter Mary. That night as I went to sleep I could hear them in the adjoining bedroom and I was angry.

After some days with them and several fishing trips with Dad I went down to Willmar to visit family. It was a good time seeing my brother Kenneth, aunts, uncles and cousins. But soon it was time to head back to Tucson and to an uncertain future.

The ROTC wanted me to continue and to become an officer in the army; ours was a cavalry unit. But I really had no home and the war was on. Besides I wanted to join the Navy; my Norsk blood was calling for the sea! Mother was confined to the hospital with no chance of an early release. The draft was taking my friends. With my parents' permission I decided to enlist.

None of the Christians gave me any particular advice. The war was on and young men had to go. A friend and i liked to take hikes and photograph the desert and the mountains. He was not a believer but was married to a woman in our fellowship. He had been in the Navy and he said to me, "Don, you are a Christian. I think you would be happier in the service helping people rather than killing them. Why don't you get in the medics?" That sounded like good advice to me as I made preparations to leave Tucson, my mother and my Christian friends.

4
Navy Days

In August 1942, I went down to the recruiting office to enlist in the Navy. First I had to pass my physical. All went well until I came to the eye test. A few years before, when I went to take my driver's test for my license, I failed the eye exam and was told, "You need glasses." I got glasses and was amazed at how much better I could see. I still remember the awe of seeing the clear Arizona sky at night filled with brilliant stars I had never noticed before! But now I had to pass a test without glasses. The army would have taken me gladly, but the Navy was more selective and was not drafting men at that time. I did not pass the Navy exam on my first try. I was really discouraged! The examiner sensed how badly I wanted to enlist and told me to rest my eyes for a bit. Then we tried again and I think he was generous and finally let me pass, although I had real difficulty with that test. The physical was quite complete and any scars were noted. Such marks could be useful in identification should one be killed in action. They recorded my weight as 156 pounds and my height as 6 1/4"! My service number was 555-63-95; my Navy identification.

Next, I must have written permission from my parents, which I hurriedly obtained. The day came when I had to say good-bye to my mother and the dear Christian friends. There were many tears. It was a scene repeated a million times in America. I did not fully appreciate at the time how devastated and lonely my mother must have felt. Her son was going off to war and she had no husband to comfort her or to care for her. She was still restricted to a frame for the sake of her back in the county hospital. More than ever she had to depend on the Lord. Those going into the Navy were hurriedly put on a bus and sent to Phoenix, where we were to be sworn in.

It was a solemn ceremony, August 28, 1942. We took an oath to be faithful, loyal and obedient in the service of our country. I realized that my life now was not my own. The Navy would control my life for some years. But I knew God would be with me and Christ was my Saviour. With God's help I knew I could live for Him and honor Him. And I believed that what I was doing was an honourable thing. Our country had been attacked and we were at war. Government authority knows the blessing of God (Rom. 13:1-7) and I felt that this was a just war. We were shipped out immediately to San Diego, where I was to enter boot camp. We went on a troop train with a steam engine belching out smoke and ash that eddied past the cars. It was a hot, tiring trip filled with apprehension over this new phase of my life. When would I see Tucson again with my mother and friends? The next day we were relieved to get to San Diego where we were picked up by buses and taken to the Naval Station.

The bus dropped us at a building where our uniforms were issued to us, along with a sea bag, hammock and thin mattress, a blanket, mattress covers, a ditty bag for toilet articles and clothes stops to use in rolling your clothes for storage. Our civilian clothes were taken from us and shipped home. I kept my Bible and a few pictures but little else. I would not wear civilian clothes again for 38 months. A Blue Jacket's Manual was given us; our Navy Bible for skills and conduct. We were told: "There is a right way to do things and a wrong way and a Navy way. We do things the Navy way." Then we were assigned to company 42-506 for training and marched off to our barracks, my new home for some weeks.

Boot camp was abbreviated because of the shortage of men in the Navy. There was a sense of urgency and pressure. Ships were being sunk and men lost at sea. New ships needed to be manned and sent off to war. There were classes on seamanship and related subjects. We were taught survival skills in the event we had to abandon ship. We even had gas mask instruction and instruction in the gas chamber. There was much marching and close order drill. Discipline and respect for authority were hammered into the men. One had to learn to obey. Once, when we failed an inspection, the company chief, whose name was Allen, was so angry that he marched us for hours under the hot, California sun until some of the men passed out. Men must learn to obey. There would come times when we would face death and our obedience was vital for the welfare of the ship and its crew. As apprentice seamen, we began at the bottom of the Navy's hierarchy! We soon came to recognize the various rates among enlisted men and the ranks among the officers.

During boot camp we were given a battery of tests. Some were then given the opportunity of specific schooling and the rest were assigned ships and stations. I guess I did well for I qualified for a school. I requested hospital corpsman school, remembering the advice of my friend in Tucson who had counseled me in that direction. But the school was full and they assigned me to quartermaster school in Newport, Rhode Island. I really did not know yet what a quartermaster did but I learned that there was little choice in the Navy during the war. They assigned you where they needed you. But looking back I was very grateful for that assignment. I discovered that a quartermaster worked on the bridge of the ship and was involved in navigation and the running of the ship. I came to love the work and the sea.

It was October 5 when we were loaded on a troop train for that long ride diagonally across the country to Newport. It was a long, exhausting trip and again we were relieved to finally arrive and to be assigned to our various schools on October 10. We arrived at the barracks that would be home for some months and settled in. Now we began to sleep in our hammocks. The hammocks were strung about five feet off the deck, a hazard if you fell out! But we were young and adapted well. Our company was 1558. A few dropped out but 132 men graduated. The school lasted for sixteen weeks.

Quartermaster school was challenging. There was much to learn: how to read a chart and make corrections if needed, how to use the various navigational instruments and keep the ship's log; a record of all of the ship's movements. We learned how to signal with semaphore and light because on smaller ships a quartermaster might be called on to do signaling as well. We had five class periods daily in semaphore, morse code and in the study of a quartermaster's duties plus three weekly periods of supervised study. There was also guard duty and work details.

We were given a liberty each week and I was able to get a picture made of me in my uniform, with hair! In boot camp they shaved our heads. I was now a Seaman 2/c. I can remember visiting the USO's recreation center for servicemen. I made a friend with a sailor from Rhode Island, who was also in the school. Henry Henault and I would be shipmates for over a year. Henry was not a Christian and I witnessed to him often. I wonder if he ever turned to God.

During that winter I was notified that my mother was dying. Her lung T.B. had become worse, the spinal involvement increased. The doctor urged me to come home immediately if I wished to see her alive. With a heavy heart I went to my commanding officer and requested an emergency leave. This was denied. It was wartime and they did not wish my schooling to be interrupted. I remember walking the streets of the base on those cold winter nights, crying out to God with tears to spare her until I could get home. As time went on she began to improve, an answer to prayer. The doctor said that it was a miracle that she recovered.

For Christmas that year Mother gave me a leather Bible with a zipper to close it and to give it protection. I carried that Bible all through my Navy days. She dated it Nov. 10, 1942, and wrote in the front of it: "Precious son. I trust that the contents of this book will be most precious to your heart all along life's journey. How we need it! May God richly bless it to your heart, that you might know Him and the power of His resurrection and the fellowship of His sufferings, being made conformable unto His death. (Phil. 3:10) My prayers will follow you everywhere you go. Tend'rest love, Mother." She had also written many verses in the front and back. She was a dear, godly mother, a woman of prayer.

Graduation was January 14, 1943, and men who had studied together for sixteen weeks now faced being scattered across the fleet. We were given a two week leave and my orders were to report to the naval base in Norfolk, Va. About half of that time was spent in travel because I had to report to Norfolk on January 30. I had a wonderful time with my mother and with the Christians at the chapel. But the time was too short and I had to leave; this time for sea duty and the war. It was a hard parting, wondering if I would ever see my mother and these friends again.

I had been assigned to the *New York BB34*, an old battleship with 14" guns. I went on board February 17 and my berthing assignment was a lower 14" handling room. She was part of the old Navy and we slept in hammocks. I was assigned to N division which was made up of quartermasters. I had the school training; now I would learn the practical side of the work.

But the Navy quickly decided that I would be transferred to a new cruiser about to be commissioned, the *U. S. S. Mobile CL 63*, and I said good-bye to the *New York BB34* on February 20, taking sea bag, hammock and all! It was kind of a Navy goof but I was glad for the opportunity to go aboard a new ship, to be part of the commissioning crew—a plank owner in Navy terms. But immediately they sent me off to 40 mm, A.A. gunnery school on the *Wyoming*, an old battleship which had become a training ship. I was trained as a quartermaster and I still do not know why they sent me to gunnery school. So I was in gunnery school for two weeks until March 6 and then I was sent back to the base to wait for the *U.S.S. Mobile*. While aboard ship I never did man a 40 mm but always functioned as a quartermaster. While in Norfolk I was able to visit the chapel in Newport News and made some dear friends. Willie and Belle Miller became special friends. Their home was open to me any time I had liberty. Belle was a motherly soul and treated me as a son. At that time they had no children of their own. I have wonderful memories of their love.

On March 24 we finally reported on board early. Commissioning ceremonies began at 9:00 a.m.. Our captain was Charles Julian Wheeler, a survivor of the *Chicago*, a heavy cruiser which had been sunk the previous year. There was a delegation from Mobile, the city for which the ship was named. After speeches were made, the command was given, "Set the watch!" The commissioning pennant was raised; the Navy band played the National Anthem and the flag was raised proudly on the fantail of the ship. The *U.S.S. Mobile* was now a commissioned Navy ship and part of the fleet.

The next weeks we were busy readying the ship to get underway on its shakedown cruise. Provisions were taken on board; ammunition was loaded and fuel tanks were filled. Finally on April 17 the ship shoved off from the pier; the engines throbbed and we were underway into Chesapeake Bay for our shakedown. The ship's crew numbered about 1,250 men and all had to learn their duties. My berthing compartment was "a foot." It was next to the chief's compartment. The quartermasters were divided into two groups, one forward and one a foot. In case one part of the ship was hit all of the quartermasters would not be lost. The quarters were tight, four bunks high, no portholes, no air conditioning, although a duct system brought in outside air.

During general quarters when the ship was battle ready every man had his battle station. My battle station was in the conning tower, which was below the bridge and was a back up command post. If the bridge was shot away, we were to take control. The main battery on this light cruiser was the twelve 6" guns with a secondary battery of ten 5". The decks also bristled with 40 mm. manned by sailors and 20 mm. AA. guns which were manned by our Marine detachment. We had 42 marines on board. We fired at targets towed by planes and targets towed by surface craft in the bay. There were various other drills, such as abandon ship. The ship was put through her paces with sharp turns and high speeds. The *U.S.S. Mobile* was 610' long, 66' beam and displaced 10,000 tons. She was a beautiful ship with a maximum speed of about 34 knots. After the shakedown we returned to port on May 18.

Before we shipped out, the assembly in Newport News had a farewell for us. Willie Smith was a local boy who had joined the Navy, and there were three other sailors leaving. It was a happy time in some ways but sad too. We wondered how many of us would survive the war. All of us did come back, except Willie. His parents grieved to their dying day. It was a time of tears and farewells.

May 30 the *U.S.S. Mobile* left for the high seas escorted by one destroyer as a submarine screen, stationed 1,000 yards ahead of us. Our destination was Portland, Maine, where we were to hold shore bombardment practice. It was exciting to be at sea, to feel the throb of the ship's engines and the roll of the sea. We were now in international waters and all hands were urged to be on the alert for periscopes or anything suspicious. Enemy submarines were active in the Atlantic. The ship was darkened at night, no exterior lights. The only light allowed topside was a flashlight with a red lens. After two days we were informed that we were going to Portland, Maine for shore bombardment.

As a quartermaster, I stood many wheel watches, learning to steer and to hold a steady course. The Portland harbor was beautiful as we entered it on June 8; it was a typical, rocky, New England coast. Two battleships were already in port, the *New York* and the *Iowa*. The next day we had gunnery practice and bombarded a small island, along with the battleships and three destroyers. It was a long day at General Quarters. In our drills we were timed to see how long it took the crew to get to battle stations and to be ready for action. The captain demanded that the ship should be ready for action in no more than six minutes. Our first drill took eleven minutes—far too slow. On June 10th we left for Boston and went into the Navy Yard for some steering gear repairs, where we spent four days; liberty was given to all. I guess I went ashore, but I don't remember much about Boston from that trip.

We had a chaplain on board, a kind man but I do not know that he was a true believer. He was more interested in lining up movies and recreation for the men than in teaching the Word. There were a few Christians on board and there were some attempts to have a Bible study. I was in the Navigator's program and was learning Bible verses and reading the Word on my own. I tried to witness some to the other quartermasters but with little success. There is tremendous pressure on men in such crowded quarters to conform. I remember witnessing to

Henry Henault but he trusted his religion as a Roman Catholic. After a wild liberty, coming back drunk, he would apologize to me the next day for his conduct.

After repairs, we left on June 15 for Panama, escorted by two destroyers. It was a beautiful, calm voyage with the sea at rest. After five days we passed south of Cuba, the sea a brilliant blue, dolphins leaping and cavorting in our wake. But the air was hot and humid; we were in the tropics. As we neared the Canal an army aircraft came out towing a target sleeve and there was gunnery practice for five hours. We arrived at Colon on June 24 and had liberty for some of the men that night. We went through the canal the following day. It took us six hours to pass through, a fascinating trip through a lush, tropical landscape. The Canal is a marvel of engineering. A pilot had come on board to guide the ship. I still remember him saying, "Steady!" as I stood a wheel watch. It was amazing to see those massive locks raise and lower the ship. There were three double sets, raising the ship 85' above sea level and then lowering it again.

We stayed one day in Balboa on the Pacific side and liberty was given to the port watch, which did not include me! The next day we got underway again after refueling. We were joined by three destroyers and a converted cruiser carrier. We headed for San Diego and went up along the coast, blessed again with calm seas. On July 1 we arrived and tied up at a pier in the beautiful harbor that is San Diego, where we refueled.

The next day we went to sea again, our destination San Francisco. On July 4 we saw the Golden Gate Bridge, always a magnificent sight, steamed under it, past Alcatraz Island and up the river to Mare Island Navy Yard, where we tied up at pier 15. We were there for two weeks for some repairs and maintenance. A recurring rudder problem had to be solved that was giving us trouble. A sailor friend I met in Norfolk had told me about the assembly in Oakland that was his home church. I looked them up and was embraced with loving arms. Mr. and Mrs. McKeone lived with their daughter Signe Richardson and they insisted I stay with them. Any time my ship was in port I had a room waiting for me. It was a bright spot in my life as a sailor. This too was where I met Bill MacDonald, who was also in the Navy at Alameda. He became a lifelong friend.

We got underway again on July 18, passing under the Golden Gate bridge, and tested the rudder with some emergency turns. The ship responded perfectly. We were on our way. After two days at sea, all hands were notified we were going to Pearl Harbor. It was a smooth voyage marked by various drills and instruction classes every day. Quartermasters were instructed in the use of a .45 caliber pistol by the marines; this was worn by the quartermaster standing watch at the gangway in port. There was great excitement when we finally sighted land and Diamond Head on July 26th. We steamed into the harbor past the wreckage of December 7, 1941, an ominous sight. Some ships were belly up, a grim reminder that we were at war. As we passed the wreckage all hands stood at attention and saluted. The ship's flag was lowered to half mast, a practice followed to this day in honor of the thousands who died that day. The salvage operation was in full swing.

For several weeks we went in and out of Pearl Harbor for gunnery practice. Mornings would begin with muster, the orders of the day and fifteen minutes of calisthenics. This would be followed with the work details. For many, this involved cleaning the ship and repairing rust spots, chipping, scraping and repainting. Rust was always a problem at sea.

Liberty was given the men when we were in port. Memories include: riding the bus into Honolulu to the Army and Navy YMCA, walking the streets and checking out the various shops, coming back from liberty with luscious pineapples, seeing long lines of men outside the houses of prostitution, getting a haircut from a woman barber and buying various souvenirs. The beach was beautiful, crowned with the famous Royal Hawaiian Hotel, now used by the Navy for rest and recreation. After one of our combat missions, I was sent there for a couple of days. Mine were clean liberties, no drinking or women; the Lord kept me clean through those service years. Liberty was usually over at midnight but I would go back to the ship much earlier. Hawaii is a tropical paradise, "where every prospect pleases and only man is vile!" Pineapple and sugar cane fields were everywhere. The fragrant smell of ripe pineapples filled the air.

We had an admiral's inspection by Admiral Chester Nimiz. For this our ship was scrubbed and spotless. As I stood at my station on the bridge, he stopped to ask me a question. He was anxious to see this newest cruiser of his fleet. I remember him as a kind man, marked with dignity and authority. We were proud to serve under him.

Finally our time in Pearl Harbour was over and we went to sea on August 21 joining task force 15 composed of a battleship, another cruiser, two carriers and about six destroyers. As we steamed westward we were told this would be a raid on Marcus Island, the closest our forces had come to Japan since Doolittle's raid. On the 30th of August we were 150 miles east of Marcus and began launching planes two hours before sunrise. The bombing continued all day with our ships moving closer to the island. Three of our planes were lost and the island was devastated. It was a partial pay back for Pearl Harbor.

The *Mobile* returned to Pearl Harbor on September 7th. After refueling, the ship got underway on the 9th and joined a larger task force composed of two other cruisers, three carriers and about nine destroyers. Our destination was Tarawa, one of the Gilbert Islands, a heavily fortified Japanese base. We arrived off the island on the 16th and launched our aircraft early in the morning. This time we lost six planes and pilots but managed to destroy their airbase and other installations. From there we headed south across the equator.

Sailors make a big deal of crossing the equator. Those who have never crossed it are "pollywogs" and must be initiated in order to become "shellbacks," members of the Ancient Order of the Deep, headed by King Neptune. The nine days previous to our crossing the equator on September 18 we pollywogs were constantly harassed and belittled by the shellbacks. Breakfast started that day with a plate filled with corn bread, scrambled eggs, oat meal and chipped beef, all mixed together! Then you had to go down a double line of men who paddled you mercilessly. Next, one had to go to the "Royal Baby," a man with a pot belly, kneel and kiss his belly, all smeared with grease! After this came the Royal Barber who cut our hair off. Then we were thrown into a tank of sea water and dunked repeatedly.

After this we crawled through a canvas tube filled with garbage while they beat on us to hurry you through. When we exited the tunnel we were blasted with a fire hose that knocked us over. Whoever survived this ordeal became a trusty shellback. But woe to the man who showed weakness!

After this we headed north to Pearl Harbor, arriving on September 24th. We refueled and took on provisions and ammunition. Our involvement was getting more intense. Less time was spent in port with less liberty. The schedule was exhausting at sea with eight hours of watch, general quarters daily and work besides. I remember feeling chronically tired. The heat also could be exhausting. I struggled to find time to read my Bible and to pray.

On September 27 we went to sea again, this time with a larger task force: four light cruisers, three heavy cruisers, three carriers, circled by ten destroyers forming a submarine screen. It was a formidable force and our target was Wake Island, now occupied by the Japanese. We surprised the enemy on October 5. For the next two days the carrier aircraft pounded the island with bombs. The heavy cruisers were on one side and the light cruisers on the other, blasting the island. Shore batteries straddled the *Mobile* with their fire but did not hit us. Some Japanese planes attacked but were shot down and two cargo vessels were sunk. The evening of the 6th we headed back to Pearl Harbor, leaving the island devastated. It was revenge for the time they took the island from us. It was an exhausting two days for the crew, constantly at their battle stations. The days en route to Pearl Harbour were a welcome rest.

We arrived at Pearl Harbour and immediately began loading stores and ammunition. This was a project that required all hands. It was hard, hot labor, until the work was finished. (I should mention that I am indebted for many of these details to Ed Buckalew, another quartermaster, who kept a diary of all of these events. Some men did keep a diary, in spite of the prohibition.) One bright spot at this time was a visit to the Royal Hawaiian. My pass read: The below named man has been granted overnight liberty for relaxation and rest at The Royal Hawaiian Hotel. Liberty expires 1600, 15 October 1943. Norbie, D.L.,

QM3/c USNR. It was quite a privilege to stay at that luxury hotel on the beautiful beach at Waikiki. I savored every moment of it, even though it was brief.

On October 30th we got underway again and joined a larger task force consisting of four battleships, four large carriers, three light cruisers, four heavy cruisers (with 8" guns) and about twelve destroyers, designated as Task Group 53.3. On November 3rd we were near the Fiji Islands, and here the three light cruisers were detached and told to proceed to Espiritu Santos in the New Hebrides. This is a beautiful harbor, and here we took on provisions and fuel and then left for the Solomon Islands. Guadalcanal was passed on our port side, the scene of bloody fighting in 1942. We stopped at Tulagi Harbor briefly to unload extra ammunition we had brought for the ships we were relieving.

On November 8th the *Mobile, Santa Fe* and *Birmingham*, all light cruisers, were off Bougainville near Empress Augusta Bay. We had relieved the three light cruisers that were covering the landings. Troop ships were busy bringing in reenforcements. All that night the Japanese attacked with dive bombers and torpedo planes in the longest night attack the *Mobile* was to know. Their planes circled around our ships like a swarm of angry hornets, dashing in periodically to drop bombs and torpedoes.

A friend in CIC (Combat Information Center) later told me he did not think we would survive the night. At least eight of their planes were shot down in the first attack and seven later. It was a long, tension-filled night, with the constant firing of our guns, the ships zigzagging and changing speed to avoid being hit. In the morning the attacks finally ceased. We were all completely exhausted after the many hours at our battle stations. Our only food was some sandwiches prepared by the galley. The *Birmingham*, our sister ship, had been hit in the bow by a torpedo and we escorted her to safety out of the battle zone. She then proceeded to Pearl Harbor for repairs with a destroyer escort. I do not know how many casualties there were. We then went back to Tulagi, a safe harbor from the heat of battle.

How does one cope with the stress of combat? When we first went into action remember seeing our chief quartermaster trying to drink a cup of coffee with a shaking hand. And I realized his heart was gripped by fear. He had been on the *Chicago* when she went down. Our captain also began having real problems in combat. Extra pants and underwear were kept on the bridge because he would soil his often. The ship's doctor stayed near him for help. He was transferred later to a station with less stress. I knew the Lord, and while there might have been a momentary surge of fear, a deep sense of peace would come. With Isaiah I could say, *"Behold, God is my salvation: I will trust and not be afraid"* (Isa. 12:2). If I should die I would be forever with the Lord. Such is the peace that faith brings.

We anchored in Tulagi the afternoon of the 10th and the ship was quickly surrounded by dugouts paddled by the natives. Young and old were begging for money to be thrown to them.They would dive to recover the coins. They wanted tobacco too—already corrupted by western ways! It was a relief to get some rest after the past days' exhausting routine. But it was a short rest. November 11th we were underway for Espiritu Santo, arriving that night. We refueled and awaited orders. Fifty bags of mail were brought on board and distributed, to the joy of all!

The next morning (12th) we went to sea again, our two cruisers, *Mobile* and *Santa Fe*, and five destroyers. We discovered we were to meet Task Force 53.7 headed for the Gilbert Islands.

We steamed at high speed to meet the convoy on November 17th. It was composed of three battleships, several transports and a number of destroyers. We were the task force that was to take Tarawa with the marines of the 2nd Division. The army with another task force was to attack Makin Island, 200 miles to the north. Tarawa was an important Japanese base, heavily fortified with a good airfield, the largest in these islands. The Japanese had rebuilt the damage we had caused in September.

On November 23rd, Thanksgiving Day, our ships moved in very early and began shore bombardment. We could hear the whoosh of the 16" shells passing over us from the battleships, and the 6" and 5" guns of the cruisers and destroyers made a deafening roar as they blasted the island. This went on for three hours before the transports moved in. The landing craft were loaded and the marines began to go ashore at about 9:30. Unfortunately, we were not informed of some of the reefs and the tides of the area. Landing craft began to go aground and the men had to wade in, some from 800 yards out, easy targets for Japanese fire. Hundreds of men were dying and being swept out to sea by the current. Two destroyers went aground on reefs and our attack was not going well. With their bunkers and gun emplacements, the Japanese had figured they could hold the island for two months under attack. At the end of the first day, the enemy was still well entrenched and we only had a small beachhead.

Ships continued to bombard the island on the second day, and the marines did better, gaining control of one half the island. After 76 hours the whole island was finally secured by the marines but it was costly. Over 1,000 marines died and over 2,500 were wounded. It was one of the worst battles of the Pacific. Bloated bodies of dead marines floated in every direction. As we patrolled around the island, we had to alter course often to keep from running them down. Our captain said, "They are our boys; don't hit any of them."

We learned from that battle that the enemy can survive in bunkers in spite of intense bombing and shelling. They could only be taken out by foot soldiers in hand-to-hand fighting. I heard later that a friend of mine from my days in Tucson had died with the marines at Tarawa, but I was unable to confirm this. I met a Christian years later in Albuquerque who had been a coxswain on one of those landing craft during that terrible battle. He survived with a grateful heart to God.

On November 30th we turned north towards the Marshall Islands and left behind that bloody scene.

DECAYING HOPES

Gray ships roll gently,
Decks piled
With spent shell casings,
Angry guns silent.
Standing my watch
I scan the sea.
Bloated, distended bags
Of human flesh,
Bursting taut skin
Bob on the heaving bosom
Of an anguished sea,
Decaying hopes ...
Brave young men
Hit that beach
Facing a storm of steel and fire
That blasted them into the sea.
Budding dreams
A business, a wife's caress, laughing children,
A life lived full
Rot,
Fueled by tropic sun.
I weep
And cling to my God.

Donald L. Norbie
March 29, 1975
U.S.S. Mobile CL 63
Tarawa, November, 1943

On December 1 the *U.S.S. Mobile* was assigned to Task Force 50 (Fast Carrier Force, Pacific Fleet). As we steamed north to the Marshall Islands. I remember hearing our captain say, "We are going into the lion's mouth!" It was strong Japanese territory. We were to attack Kwajalein and Wotje. Early on December 4th, we were 200 miles off the islands and the attack began with the carriers launching their aircraft. The battle went on all day with some Japanese torpedo planes attacking us, but they were shot down. We were at our battle stations all night under constant Japanese attack. All that night our ship was turning, changing speed and firing at the incoming planes.

Early on the morning of the 5th, one of our 5" guns malfunctioned and fired into a 40 mm. mount, killing two men and critically injuring twenty-two. I still remember going down to Sick Bay and smelling the sickening odor of burned flesh. It was a tragedy that affected us all. The *U.S.S. Mobile* was often called "The Lucky Mobile" because she was never hit by enemy fire. Other ships with us would be hit but she was unscathed and went through much action, receiving 13 battle stars for her service.

Because of that accident, the ship was detached from the task force and ordered back to Pearl Harbor for repairs. It was a solemn voyage, carrying our dead and wounded. As we entered the harbor our flag was flying at half mast. A Navy band was playing at the pier. Ed Buckalew wrote in his diary, "I can assure you that last deployment was no pleasure cruise. Everyone from the Captain on down were really on edge, or what we called "war nerves." The wounded were sent to a hospital, the dead buried and repairs begun on the ship.

A third of the crew was sent ashore to a rest camp for a couple of days of relaxation. It was known as Camp Andrew at Nanakuli Beach. We stayed in small cabins which were named after the various states. Each cabin had two cots. It was a time of relaxation with some sports and for many beer drinking. I myself enjoyed the beautiful beach with its booming surf. It was a restful two days.

Then I discovered that I was in for a change. Several of us had taken the exam for QM 3/c and I was the one who had passed the test and was given the rate on September 1st , but the rate was in excess of complement. That meant I would likely be transferred to another ship. When I came back to the ship my orders were waiting. I was transferred December 11th to go back to San Francisco for new construction. I hated to leave the *Mobile* and the men I had come to know. She was a great ship. But in the wartime Navy you did not choose your assignment. I wondered, "What ship will I get next?" It was a sad day when I packed my sea bag and left the ship. I said goodbye to Henry Henault and the rest of my shipmates in N Division. Then I went aboard the *Indianapolis* (CA-35) for the trip back to the States. Little did I know that the *Indianapolis* would be the last ship sunk by the Japanese with tremendous loss of life at the end of the war. General Robert E. Lee of Civil War fame said, "It is good that war is so terrible or men would love it too much."

Navy Days

LIFE IS A MOUNTAIN

U.S.S. Mobile April 1943

U.S.S Salamaua CVE 96

WM. B. Preston AVD7

5

A Carrier and a Destroyer

After saying good-byee to my friends on the *U.S.S. Mobile*, I went briefly to the Base at Pearl Harbor, then aboard the *Indianapolis* for the trip back to San Francisco. I was in charge of six other men being transferred from the *Mobile*. We got underway on December 13 from Pearl Harbor. The voyage was uneventful. The weather was good and I spent some time on the bridge assisting the quartermaster. The Golden Gate Bridge was a most welcome sight after the months overseas. It is one of the most beautiful bridges in the world, a majestic span over the channel. The ship was tied up and I went to the Receiving Station in San Francisco with the six men in my charge on December 18.

It was great to be back in the bay area and I had some good times at the Bethany assembly in Oakland and with the McKeones and Signe. They were very kind to me, and it was great to be in their home and to enjoy their loving hospitality. What a blessing Christian fellowship is! Aboard ship I had very little. My orders came through on January 15th, 1944, and I was transferred to the Receiving Station in Bremerton, Washington, for assignment to the *U.S.S. Salamaua* (CVE 96), a small carrier. I was to report on February 4th, so had a good leave. It was wonderful to see the Christians in Tucson again and to be with my mother. She was delighted to see me and very proud of her Navy son. There is no love like a mother's! Her back had healed and her condition improved, so she was now in a rest home. But too soon I had to report back to the Navy. I guess I rode the Greyhound bus, my usual mode of transportation to Tucson.

After checking in there was not too much to do for several weeks, so I applied myself to studying for the next rate. On March 1st, I made QM 2/c and was thankful for that promotion. It meant an increase in my pay and more of a dependent's allowance for my mother. I was in Bremerton for some weeks awaiting the completion of my ship. It was a good opportunity to meet the Christians at the assembly in Seattle who met at Hope Gospel Hall. I rode the ferry over many times. They were very kind to me and I was in several homes for meals. It was a spiritual oasis. The Andersons and the Flemings were especially kind to me. Peter and Ken Fleming were in high school then, I believe. Both went on to become missionaries and Peter was killed in Ecuador by the Waorani (Auca) Indians in 1956. Their grandfather was Inglis Fleming, a venerable, godly man, the author of some beautiful hymns.

Finally my orders came to transfer to Astoria, Oregon for the pre-commissioning detail. I was transferred on April 19 and immediately became involved in preparing the charts for the new ship. These had to be brought up to date with all the changes that had been made in navigational aids, such as buoys, etc. It was tedious and painstaking work, writing with a fine-pointed, mapping pen, but it had to be done. It was a very busy time; the ship would soon be commissioned and we had to be ready.

We reported on board May 26th, 1944, and the ship was commissioned. Once again I was a "plank owner." Captain Joseph Taylor was our captain. We had our shake down cruise in Puget Sound and then loaded damaged aircraft and parts in Seattle and went to Alameda where we loaded more parts. From there we went down to San Diego on July 29 and unloaded. This was followed by some practice runs, launching and recovering aircraft. The *Salamaua* was a "baby flattop carrier," designed primarily for escort work. Later these ships were used to back up invasions in the Pacific. She was 512 feet long with a beam of 65 feet and was built on a cargo hull by Kaiser. These ships could be built quickly and cheaply and we built a lot of them. But they were slow, 19 knots maximum speed, and vulnerable. They only had a 5 inch gun and some 40 mm. and 20 mm. A. A. She was manned by 860 officers and men. After being on a cruiser it was definitely a second class ship and I missed the cruiser.

Our first overseas mission was to transport a load of planes to Pearl Harbor. We left San Diego on July 6th and arrived in Pearl Harbor on July 12th where we unloaded the aircraft and passengers. We then put to sea again and returned to Alameda on July 22nd. We loaded up, this time with 50 new aircraft and 300 naval passengers. Now we were bound for Finschafen, New Guinea. July 24th we went to sea again, passing under the Golden Gate Bridge, always a magnificent sight. Our voyage was uneventful and on August 3rd we crossed the equator and had the customary initiation. Now I was a shellback and could harass the pollywogs! We also crossed the date line which makes one a qualified Golden Dragon, whatever that means! New Guinea was a typical, tropical island, lush and green. We arrived on August 12th, tied up at the new dock, unloaded the aircraft and passengers but only had time for a beer party on the beach. I was standing watch on the quarterdeck and helped drunk sailors back aboard, including our Roman Catholic chaplain. Such was our spiritual leadership.

We loaded damaged aircraft and set our course for the United States on August 14th. The ship arrived in Alameda, California on September 1 where we took on additional cargo. We then left for San Diego where the ship was scheduled to go into the Naval Repair Base for maintenance.

The chief quartermaster had taken an aversion to me, perhaps because of my witnessing to him and the men. I was not too happy on the ship and requested a transfer, which was seldom granted. But I think the chief wanted me off the ship and I was transferred September 12 to CASU 11 at Port Hueneme. I had no idea what this was; I had hoped for another cruiser. It was Carrier Aircraft Support Unit 11, a group of men that would go in after an island was taken and set up a base for our planes. We were all issued marine clothes and I functioned basically like a boatswain's mate, handling men and driving a jeep around the base. We lived in tents like marines.

I was frustrated. My rate was a seagoing rate, trained for

navigation. It was another Navy goof. I was an unhappy sailor and I realized that I should have been content on the *Salamaua* and tried to get along with that chief. I prayed about it and said, "Lord, if you get me on another ship, I will try to be content." I talked to some of the officers and, lo and behold, they transferred me again on October 23rd! I was not sorry to leave that station.

I should add that the *Salamaua* went on to see action at Lingayen Gulf where she was hit by a kamikaze on January 13th, 1945. The plane crashed on the flight deck; the bomb exploded and much damage was done. Fifteen men were killed and eighty were wounded. Power, communication and steering failed. The ship's gunners managed to down two other kamikaze planes in that battle. Temporary repairs enabled the ship to return to San Francisco. Repairs were quickly made and she returned to action in the Pacific. She earned three battle stars for her service and was decommissioned on May 19, 1946, having served her country well. Later that year she was scrapped, as was the *Mobile*, an ignominious end for great ships.

Of these carriers Admiral Chester Nimitz said: "The story of the escort aircraft carriers is like a story with a surprise ending. When the United States began to build them, there was a definite purpose in view, fighting off submarines and escorting convoys. But as the war progressed, the small carrier demonstrated surprising versatility. It became a great more than its name implies. From a purely defensive measure, the escort carrier emerged as an offensive weapon." Six CVEs were sunk during the war, one in the Atlantic and five in the Pacific.

Now where would I go? I was transferred to the Receiving Station, Camp Elliott, San Diego. From my records I see I had grown a little, now 6'1" and 170 pounds! Another leave was given me from November 2nd to 18th, and I went back to Tucson again to see my mother and Christian friends. Then it was back to San Diego and a wait for my next ship. While there I had good fellowship with the believers who met at the chapel on Marlborough Street. They were very active in reaching out to sailors with the gospel and with Christian hospitality. Guy and Margaret Horton took me in, along with some other sailors. On liberty I could always go to their home in National City for

A CARRIER AND A DESTROYER

some home cooking and loving hospitality.

There was an old destroyer in the harbor, just returned from duty in Australia where she had served as a destroyer seaplane tender. She was the *Wm. B. Preston*, an old flush deck destroyer, also called a four piper. These ships were built between 1917 and 1922. They were 314 feet long with a beam of 31 feet. They were quite fast; one set a record at the time of 40 knots. Some had served valiantly in WWI and some were scrapped but 169 survived for WWII. Fifty of them were traded to the UK for bases in the western hemisphere in 1940. A German sub sank the *Reuben James*, *DD245*, about a month before Pearl Harbor, the first war ship we lost in the war. At Pearl Harbor, two of these destroyers sank two Japanese submarines attempting to enter the harbor. They served in various functions as mine sweepers, as high speed transports, seaplane tenders and regular destroyers. They served valiantly in the war earning 422 battle stars, 21 Presidential Unit Citations and 94 Navy Unit Commendations. Men on them earned medals from the Medal of Honor to the Purple Heart. Unfortunately none remain today; all were scrapped.

The *Wm. B. Preston* was commissioned as DD 344, August, 23, 1920, and saw much service in the far east. Because of naval treaties, the U. S. had to decommission some ships from 1934 to 1940, among them DD 344. In 1940 she was recommissioned as AVD 7. She was sent from the east coast to Pearl Harbor and became part of the Pacific fleet. When the war began she fought her way from the Philippines down to Australia where a Japanese attack on Darwin nearly destroyed her. Eleven men were killed, two missing and two wounded. There was heavy bomb damage in the stern of the ship. But she survived and after repairs continued to serve in that area. She finally came back to the States September 18, 1944, and had massive repairs and an overhaul in San Pedro. Now she was in San Diego, her new home port. She was to be my last ship in the Navy; I went aboard December 9th,1944.

It was a different type of duty. The quarters were tight and there were few amenities, (for example, no laundry). We washed our own clothes by hand. The man I was replacing showed me around the ship. His name was Carter and he was a QM1/c; he had served on her when she was in Australia. I would be the lead quartermaster, and he told me my duties before he left the ship. I would bunk in the after berthing compartment, near the screws, a noisy place when you were underway. The ship's crew numbered about 125, so one became acquainted with all. Each berthing compartment had a table and the men in that compartment ate together. A man was designated as the mess sailor and would go to the galley to get the food in pots and bring it to the compartment. He also did the clean up. The ship was rough riding. She sat low in the water and in heavy seas water flooded all over the deck. I soon adjusted and fit in. I was determined to stay with this ship and I came to have affection for her, even though I still missed the cruiser.

Our duty was to function as an antisubmarine escort ship, using our sonar, and a plane guard for carriers along the west coast. These small carriers were qualifying carrier pilots, and our job was to pick up any pilots who ditched their planes while training. Whenever we sent a pilot back that we had picked up, the carrier would send over a tub of ice cream in appreciation. We operated with a number of the smaller carriers and were often in San Diego, but at times in the Bay area.

One morning I was coming back from liberty in Oakland and traffic held us up. I finally got to the base and dashed to the ship. She was just getting underway and I had to jump to get aboard. I hurriedly ran to the bridge to take over the wheel, my post as we got underway. The captain scowled at me and said, "Don't do that again!" But I was not disciplined. To miss ship is a cardinal sin. Later we were in a storm off San Francisco, and I almost thought we might lose the ship. She was rolling 45 degrees. I stood on the fan tail as we slid down into a trough of the sea and looked up at walls of water on each side. It was awesome; God was flexing His muscles! We had some damage to the bridge structure from that storm and had to go into port for repairs. She was a tough old ship and I became fond of her. There is a bond between sailors and their ships!

I took my tests for QM 1/c and passed them. I received my rate May 1st and was happy for the additional pay and responsibility. When we came into San Diego we would often tie up to a buoy, and when liberty was announced water taxis would come by the ship to take men ashore. I would usually head for the Hortons and spend my time there and at the assembly. At times I would stop at the YMCA and work out on my way. I have good memories of San Diego and of the assembly of believers there.

But then the atomic bombs were dropped and the war came to an abrupt end on August 15th. Now the *Preston* was assigned to go to the east coast for decommissioning. Our captain asked me to stay on board to take her around through Panama to the east coast; he promised if I would do this, that he would promote me to chief. It was tempting but I wanted to get out and to get on with my life. I had plenty of points for a quick discharge. On October 5th I was transferred to Camp Elliott in San Diego to await discharge. It was with mixed emotions that I said goodbye to the crew, packed my sea bag and one last time saluted the flag at the stern as I left the ship. I loved the sea and my work. What would my future hold?

LIFE IS A MOUNTAIN

Donald and Marys' (Marie) wedding June 1947

Myrtle Viola Norbie (My Mother) (last picture 1945)

6

COLLEGE YEARS AT WESTMONT

After arriving at Camp Elliott I was processed rather quickly for discharge, and on October 15 I received my final papers and left the base. My Navy career was over and I was a free man. It was kind of a weird feeling, not having to report back for duty. No longer would Uncle Sam control my every move; I had to make decisions on my own, hopefully with the Lord's guidance.

I went to the Hortons for the last time, said goodbye and Margaret very kindly took me out to the highway heading east to Yuma. She later told me she hated to leave me there on the road alone. She was a motherly soul and wept a little. I had good success catching rides. People were quick to pick up servicemen during the war years. Soon I was in Tucson and saw my mother again. I had been thinking of going back to college but the fall semester had already started for most schools. Should I wait and go back to the University of Arizona for the spring semester? The GI Bill was going to help servicemen finish their education.

Some friends from Tucson were going to a small Christian college in California named Westmont. The school had moved from Los Angeles to Santa Barbara that summer and the fall semester was starting late. If I hurried I could enroll and get going on my education. My mother was in favor of my going there; she always wanted my best. I could get back to Tucson quite often. She still was confined to a rest home and was a bed patient most of the time. I hurriedly contacted the school and they urged me to come. Once again it was good-byee to the Tucson folk and off to Santa Barbara.

The war had finished earlier in Europe and some army men were already discharged and at school. There were some young people just out of high school but there were many fresh out of the service, mature, serious and wanting to live for God. Looking back I realize what a great group of men they were. The current college scene with its partying is quite a contrast. I was quickly enrolled and went into the sophomore class. With summer school I made up a semester and graduated in three and a half years from college.

The college had purchased a couple of estates and was converting these to class rooms and dorm rooms. The school was in a beautiful setting in Montecito, a rather exclusive area of Santa Barbara. It was high in the foothills and the mountains rose up in back of the college, very picturesque. I shared a big room with four other men who were just out of high school. I was used to sharing quarters so it was no problem for me. I put a small baby picture of myself on my dresser. When they asked about this I told them it was a picture of my son in Australia! This caused a bit of consternation. What was this salty sailor doing at Westmont, a Christian college? In time I told them the truth and they settled down. But there was quite a gap between the servicemen and the high school students in maturity. The servicemen were disciplined and serious. This set the tone for the school.

To help augment my GI bill I worked around the campus. For a while I drove a bus for the school and later worked as a gardener. The grounds were beautifully landscaped and we wanted to keep them looking good. To work with the soil was a good break from studying. I took liberal arts courses and decided to major in Greek, the language of the New Testament. I minored in history and English. An orientation course at the beginning was a help to me in organizing my studies. The military had organized my life before; now I must discipline myself and use my time wisely. They encouraged the scheduling of your time by hours with two hours of study for each hour of class. It worked for me; I stayed on top of my studies and never had to cram for finals.

I went back to Tucson for Christmas and enjoyed the time with Christian friends and my mother. Mr. Gilbert had married a Tucson lady and now lived in Tucson again. It was great to spend some time with them. But I sensed things were not going so well for my mother.

I went back to school and got busy in my studies and work. I had been elected as one of the class officers and also was active as a photographer for the school annual. Our sophomore class numbered about fifty, as I recall. It was a busy, happy life. The service men had a club on campus and it sent out teams to speak at the various churches. I began doing more speaking. Since there was no assembly along New Testament lines in Santa Barbara I began going to Calvary Baptist Church and became quite active. Wanting to encourage me, they licensed me to preach and I led the college age group.

But in mid-semester I was called back to Tucson. My mother was doing poorly and it was decided she must go to a state hospital. It was a hard decision, but her condition continued to deteriorate until she died in September; delusional and confused at the end. She was only forty-two years old and had been ill and bedridden over half of her life. When I think of all the sorrow and pain she knew in life I could weep. Dear mother! She was a godly, loving woman and my memories of her are sacred. Her body is buried in Evergreen Cemetery in Tucson, a lovely setting with the majestic Santa Catalina Mountains as a back drop. But her spirit is with the Lord, thank God!

I finished the spring semester, having dated several girls at the school. The spring banquet was held the night before graduation and I still had not decided to date a girl. Several of us decided to date several of the senior girls. They suggested that I ask Edna Marie Adams to go with me. Several of us couples sat together at the banquet and then decided to go out together; Dick Bohrer, one of the men, had a car. So we walked the beach, went up by a light house and marveled at the beauty of the sea. And we talked and talked and ate at a restaurant. I found myself enjoying the company of this girl. When we finally said good night it was late, too late. I think we would have been in trouble with the school but we were all good students and they let it pass.

The next day was graduation and Eddie, her nick name, graduated. That might have ended the matter, but I decided to keep in touch. She wrote in my annual after that night, "Food, fellowship and foolishness and sunrise. Please let me know next time you feel like completely unbending and I'll come flying. Thanks for topping off my Westmont days in such a delightful way." It sounds like something got started! I visited her at her home in Rosemead, California, and also at the Christian camp in the mountains where she worked as a cook. During the summer I made a trip back to Minnesota to see relatives, catching a ride with other students. Before I left she gave me a picture of herself, saying, "I don't want you to forget me. I know there are some cute Scandinavian girls in Minnesota!"

Before leaving the Navy I visited the PX store and noticed they had jewelry at reasonable prices. I saw a diamond ring that I liked. I said to myself, "Why not buy it for the time you will want to marry?" So I did. That summer I visited her at the camp several times. One night we walked out among the pines and sat down on a huge rock, still warm from the heat of the sun and watched the stars. We talked a while and then I reached over and took her left hand and slipped the ring on her finger. It fit perfectly. It was completely unexpected and she was shocked but by then she had come to love me and agreed to the engagement. We both wanted to live for God and to please Him.

She had a teaching job that fall up in the valley near Tulare, California, and roomed with a college friend, Adeline Stineberg, a Jewish Christian. In the fall she came down and with college friends we went out to a restaurant for dinner. It was there that we publicly announced our engagement, planning to marry the next summer.

That year was a very busy year. I dropped out of some campus activities, such as working on the annual. Besides my studies, work, and church activities I now made frequent trips up the valley to see my wife-to-be. Harry Rosenberg, a friend at school, was interested in Adeline and we would hitchhike together. It was the fastest way to get there and we had some interesting rides and opportunities to witness to people. During the year Harry and Adeline also became engaged and were married the next summer. Harry went on to get a PhD and became a history professor.

Several other students became interested in starting a meeting for the Breaking of Bread or Lord's Supper on Sunday evenings. Bill Howell, a student from Iowa and came from an assembly there. So several of us began to meet together in a simple way to remember our Lord. Other students became interested as well as a few faculty members. I felt we should also have morning meetings but some wanted to be free to go to other churches in the morning. This was the status when we graduated and left the area. Later the fellowship did expand its program.

Finally school was over We were married on Saturday, June 7, 1947, in San Gabriel, California, at a large independent church that her family attended, San Gabriel Union Church. Mr. King, a professor at Westmont and a dear Christian man, married us. It was a frugal wedding. Marie, as I began to call her, and her mother made her wedding. The reception was held in the backyard of her home. We had no car so at the conclusion of the reception Mr. Winters, her principal, took us to our hotel room in his car. We were now married and began to live together as man and wife. Next we caught a train from Los Angeles at 12:15 up the coast to San Luis Obispo, a beautiful, scenic ride along the Pacific Ocean with the mountains hugging the beach. We stayed Sunday night in San Luis Obispo and the next day we rambled around the town and enjoyed seeing the historic old mission. We then took a bus down to Pismo Beach in the afternoon and rented a room in the Butler Hotel. But on Wednesday we moved over to an inexpensive motel room in Adams' Court! It had a little kitchen so we could prepare our own meals most of the time. We were low on funds and had to economize! But it was a great week with perfect weather for that long, beautiful, white beach. We dug clams every day; Pismo is famous for its clams. Marie cooked them every way she could imagine and I discovered I was married to a good cook. We determined also to read the Word of God together and to pray daily, a practice we have maintained all of our married life.

But the week was too short and we had to catch a bus on June 14th and go back to Santa Barbara and summer school for me. Mr. and Mrs Reynolds had an estate next to the campus and a student couple had stayed with them the year before. Since they were leaving, we applied for that position. It would mean room and board with a little salary. Marie would be their cook and housekeeper and I would do yard maintenance. They had been wealthy at one time and still had many fashionable friends who would come for tea and meals. Marie learned how to entertain very graciously and was a favorite of Mrs. Reynolds'. I had many talks with them about the gospel but they were not open at that time. They were good, cultured people and felt no sense of need for salvation. Later we understand Mrs. Reynolds did turn to the Lord. We were very thankful for this provision of the Lord for our needs.

Mr. Reynolds raised flowers as a hobby and also commercially. He also had a flock of sheep and he knew them by name. One lamb lost its mother, killed by dogs, and we raised it on a bottle. We called it Limlamb and it followed Marie around like a puppy. When the time came to slaughter some of the lambs I was asked to help the butcher who came out. He cut their throats with a sharp knife and they bled to death quietly with no resistence. I was moved by the experience and Isaiah 53 came alive to me. What a picture of our Saviour's death!

Some things in the Baptist Church were troubling me. My experience earlier in an assembly along New Testament lines was embedded in my thinking. I decided we needed to come to some convictions about the church. I felt called of God to preach His Word but with which church should I cast my lot?

Earlier a friend in Oakland had told me, "Don, don't go into full time work with assemblies. It is too hard. Teach in a university instead." I had done some interdenominational work and that had a certain appeal. That ministry had a wide field but I knew too that one's teaching would be limited. One had to be careful about offending the various churches.

We decided it was time to study the Word and make some

decisions. We came from different traditions and needed to get our thinking together. We worked our way through the New Testament, studying all the passages that have reference to the church. We did careful exegesis and wrote down our conclusions. It brought our thinking together and we both felt constrained to follow the simple pattern of the early church. I went to see the pastor, Dr. Goodfield, a dear, gentle, old man. I explained to him some of my problems with the Baptist Church. There were things that troubled him too but he said, "Don, you are young so you can leave. I am old and have my retirement to look forward to." The church was sorry to see us go and, I think, was perplexed about it all. What kind of sect were these people getting into?

In November I applied to Wheaton Graduate School. I had heard about their M.A. program where I could get some more Greek, Hebrew and related studies. I did not want to go through a typical seminary program which would take three years. With hard work I believed I could finish Wheaton in one year and academically it was very good. In January we started to help a little American Sunday School Union work in a small community called Casmalia. We had our meetings in an old Quonset hut and worked the community with tracts and visitation. Several other students worked with us.

I had been having colds and flu all winter. The doctor discovered my tonsils had grown back and were diseased. In February I had my tonsils removed again and spent several days recuperating. Marie was a loving nurse. It did put me behind in school so I had to work hard to catch up. I also had work to do for Mr. Reynolds, sawing wood, painting buildings and doing yard work. It was a busy year.

In April we bought our first car, a 1941 Studebaker Champion for $825.00. It needed work but we were young and willing. It turned out to be more of a project than we had thought. We later had to put a rebuilt engine in it, redo the interior and sand it for painting. As the Spanish say, *"Mucho trabajo!"* Now we were able to use it for the drive to Casmalia. The Lord was blessing our efforts. On April 18 we had 43 out and four young people gave their testimonies. Sunday afternoons we would drive back for the evening Breaking of Bread in Santa Barbara.

May 30 was our last day to go to Casmalia. We said goodbye to the Christians and had to commit them to the Lord. It had been a pioneering venture, our first in our marriage. Now there was much work as we prepared to leave Westmont. We had to finish work on the car. The last job was sanding it; then it was ready to be painted. There was the concluding study for my final exams. Finally on Saturday, June 12, was graduation, and my wife was elated that I graduated with high honor. There were final, tearful goodbys as we separated from dear Christians we had been with for three years. Now we were scattering to the four winds. Would we ever see one another on earth again?

7
A Busy Year At Wheaton

After graduation we were headed for Wheaton, Illinois, and summer school. But we discovered we had too much stuff for our little car. We bought a one wheel trailer in Rosemead on Monday, June 14, loaded it, and returned to Rosemead. We repacked the trailer, said goodbye to the folks and finally left at 1:00 a.m.! It was crazy but we drove all night and missed some of the hot desert. In Arizona we turned off at Wickenburg to go north to Prescott. But the car could not pull the trailer up that mountain grade above Congress. We came back to Congress to the railroad station and shipped 200 lbs back to Illinois.

With a hot desert tailwind the car heated often so we had to make frequent stops on that steep grade. We finally made it to Prescott and rented a motel room. A good night's sleep was such a blessing. We visited around Prescott, saw my old house and grade school. That brought back many happy memories.

Then it was off to the Grand Canyon where we drove around to soak in the spectacular views. We camped overnight in a park camp ground. We were trying to see as much as possible on our way east. The North Rim of the Grand Canyon was delightful with its pines and crisp mountain air. From there we drove to Zion National Park and camped there, enjoying the massive rock formations and the rushing, clear river. Next it was to Bryce National Park with its spectacular, red rock formations.

We pressed on north and camped east of Salt Lake City. The

next day we had the car serviced there. We walked around the Temple Square and saw the Mormon Tabernacle.

Beautiful buildings housing a false religion! Here we decided to sell the trailer since it was now empty and we needed the money.

We drove on north through Idaho and camped about twenty miles west of Yellowstone. I slept outside but Marie slept in the car, a cold night! Marie wrote in her diary that I was frozen and cross! We drove in the West Entrance about 7:00 a.m. and spent the day driving around and taking in all the sights of that amazing park with its geysers and boiling pots. Marie was ecstatic. We also saw moose and bear and left the park at the south entrance that evening.

The roads were terrible south of Yellowstone, full of potholes and rocks. We finally pulled off the road and slept in the car during a heavy rain. We drove on but the car was making strange noises and we were praying we would make it to Laramie, Wyoming. We made it. Praise the Lord! The car broke down in the center of Laramie and we had it towed to a garage. They told us the differential housing had been broken due to the rough roads.

More delays, and it was now June 21, and we needed to get to Wheaton for classes. We had to lay over in a motel that night while the car was repaired. We had a hot meal, our first since leaving home! We had been eating lots of cold lunches and had a box of avocados from Reynolds. We had to lay over another day while they fixed the car and we were able to wire the bank for some money. This trip was going to be expensive. Finally the car was ready on the 23rd and we left for Pine Bluffs and Marie's Aunt Ruth's home, arriving about 6:45 p.m.. After supper and a good visit we left at 9:00 p.m., needing to drive all night to make up time.

I started driving and drove east to N. Platte while Marie slept. Then she started driving and I slept. About 4:15 am. I awakened with the car rolling over and our belongings tumbling about. I guess Marie was screaming. We came to rest on our left side in a ditch. I managed to push the car door up and open and climbed out. Then I pulled Marie out and we took inventory. This was in the days when there were no seat belts in cars but amazingly we were unhurt. Marie was pregnant with our first child but she seemed all right. We fervently thanked God.

A Greyhound bus had stopped and the driver rushed over, a very frightened man. The highway was narrow and Marie had gotten off on a soggy, wet shoulder. She pulled back on the highway too rapidly and was heading straight for that Greyhound bus! Then she swerved to the right, lost control and the car rolled over and slid down into the ditch. No wonder the bus driver was shaken! We climbed into the bus and he took us to the nearest town, Gothenburg, Nebraska.

We were able to call a wrecker and he took us back to the wreck. After pulling it upright he towed the car back to town to a garage. The damage was extensive. The left fenders and side were smashed in and the side windows were broken. We had to wait until 7:30 a.m. for the garage to open and to evaluate the damage. The axle was broken; wheels were bent and a brake drum was cracked. Besides this there was all the body damage. Haste makes waste! We would have been wiser to stay over and sleep in Pine Bluffs. But we were thankful we were not hurt. The Lord had watched over us.

The garage had to send to Omaha for parts so it meant we would have to stay over that night. We rented a motel for $3.50 and slept part of the afternoon. Dead tired! We got up to eat supper. Marie noted that we had a delicious, hamburger steak dinner for $0.60! We had a good night's sleep and a good breakfast at our little restaurant. The car was finally ready at 12:30 p.m. and we were on our way again. They beat out the sheet metal so we could drive the car. We had put so much time and energy into that car; it was our pride and joy. Now it was a wreck. Maybe the Lord was trying to teach us how uncertain possessions can be.

We drove on across Nebraska and into Iowa and kept driving all night. I did most of the driving. Finally we arrived at 9:00 a.m. at Glen Ellyn, where we were to stay with a Christian family. They showed us two small rooms to live in, and we began to wonder if this arrangement would work out. Marie was to help around the house for our rent. We hauled our belongings in and that afternoon I went to Wheaton to register for summer school. We were utterly exhausted that night and slept soundly. After getting settled we put the car in a body shop to get repaired.

Summer school kept me busy. Because Westmont was not accredited yet, Wheaton required me to do a semester of under graduate work. I enjoyed the subjects, the Minor Prophets and History of the Renaissance and Reformation, and did well so that they allowed me to apply for the graduate school. We were getting adjusted to the hot, humid summers of Illinois. Over July 4 we went down to southern Illinois for an Adams' family reunion. There were lots of new faces and names to remember.

Back in Glen Ellyn things did not go well. Marie was having morning sickness with her pregnancy and too much work was expected of her. We began to meet with the Christians at Bethany House in Wheaton and enjoyed a warm welcome. The assembly had bought a large older house and then built on a commodious room for meetings. Mr. and Mrs. Harold Harper lived upstairs and helped with the work.

We decided we needed to live by ourselves and found a room for rent, sharing a kitchen with Mr. and Mrs. Loptson, returned missionaries from the Philippines, lovely people. We moved in on July 13 to Marie's great relief! Because this house was used as a Christian school during the year, we had to move again at the end of August. I took a part time job, working at a grocery store.

While parked at the curb on a trip to Chicago a truck sideswiped us, and kept on going. We drove madly after him and finally managed to stop him. We got his name and insurance company information and were able to get the car repaired at their expense. That car! We decided to sell it, get a cheaper car and possibly buy a trailer for housing. We picked up a model A Ford for $125.00 and got a buyer for our car. Marie began to go to a doctor and discovered his fee for prenatal care and delivery was $100.00. She was able to get a part time job as a cashier at the school dining hall; this would help our finances. Later we fixed up the Model A and sold it for $160.00 and bought a Model B Ford with a V-8 engine for $195.00! The body was rusted out in places but the engine ran well and was powerful, our hot rod.

My wife accused me of becoming a used car dealer.

The last week of August we decided to take a trip to Minnesota to visit my family. Marie had never met any of them. Dad and May gave us a friendly reception. We enjoyed seeing Duluth with its scenic harbor. Lake Superior is so large that it is almost like an ocean. Dad and I did some fishing on Rice Lake and Big Lake and I had some opportunities to witness to him. But he was still blind to his own need of salvation. We were able to visit U. S. Steel where Dad worked; very fascinating.

Then it was off to Willmar and visits with the rest of the relatives. At a family reunion for the Norbies I asked my grandmother if I could speak a few minutes. I preached the gospel and told them my testimony, with a burdened heart for their salvation. But there was little response; their religion had deadened any sense of need. I also had an opportunity to speak at a Carlson gathering, telling them of my mother's and my conversion. There were tears as they remembered my mother, their beloved sister.

We left for school on September 7th and had a safe trip to Wheaton. When I had applied for graduate school they told me the courses were full and urged me to apply to some other school or seminary. There was no way I could go to Wheaton that year. But I told them we felt the Lord had led us here and we had no interest in going to another school. Upon arriving back in town we were informed I was accepted as a full time student! Praise the Lord! An answer to prayer. Marie began working the noon and evening meals at Williston Dining Hall. School started and I was busy with a heavy load of classes. We began to go to the town of Warrenville Sunday afternoons for a children's class that was beginning. We usually had around fifteen children come. This work developed into a healthy assembly later.

We heard various speakers at Bethany that broadened our horizon. Dr. Northcote Deck, who had worked as a missionary in the Solomon Islands, was one of these. One Sunday Bill McCartney took me along to share a meeting at Fernwood Gospel Chapel on the south side of Chicago. Bill was one of the elders at Bethany and took an interest in us. The fall colors were fascinating for us as the leaves turned brilliant reds, yellows and oranges. Marie noticed the baby moving on October 6 and was excited. New life was stirring!

Finally on October 21, having received the car title from California, we were able to sell the Studebaker for $600.00 and bought a 1936 Chevrolet. We sold the 1932 Ford and the Chevy ran faithfully all winter, starting on the coldest days. With the money we now had we were able to buy a 1942 trailer, 25 feet long, and had it moved out north of town on the back of a big lot. We paid cheap rent and had an outhouse and no water in the trailer but we did have electricity. It was not luxurious but it served our needs and Marie made it homey. Over the foot of our bed was a small bunk, just right for our baby to come. The main problem I had was cold feet; that floor was frigid all winter. We were able to take showers at the school gym.

I began having rectal problems and went to Marie's doctor for an exam. He said I needed surgery and scheduled it for November 20 at the Geneva hospital. The surgery recovery kept me in the hospital until the 24th. The hospital bill was $56.00 and the Lord had enabled us to pay all of the bills. Then it was home and the loving care of my wife. The doctor urged Marie to quit work because of some early contractions, which meant we would eat all our meals now at home.

Jim Elliott and I had become friends and he visited us at times, in our trailer, for meals. The quarters were cramped but we loved to entertain guests and Marie was an excellent cook. We went caroling with Jim and the other young people from the Lombard Chapel at Christmas time. It was a very cold night but beautiful with fresh, clean snow. It was all a new experience for people who had recently come from California. Jim was passionate in his concern for foreign missions and he motivated many to have more concern for the lost overseas. He later went to Ecuador and gave his life in the service of our Lord. We kept in touch until his death. He was a dear friend and a man of God.

Studies took up much time. I took a heavy load of Greek, Hebrew and theological studies. All year I was busy writing papers and Marie would type them for me. Their M. A. program usually took two years to finish but I felt I could finish it in a year and write my thesis as well. January 8 I drove into Chicago to Emmaus Bible School at 69th and Normal streets Bill MacDonald, a friend from Navy days, was teaching there. The Emmaus work in Chicago was just starting and Ed Harlow wanted to talk with me about helping with the teaching in Toronto Emmaus, the parent school. Ed was the principal there. We were to pray about the matter. On January 13 Marie noted that she had gained 19 pounds and the pregnancy was going well. The baby was due the first part of February. I was asked to begin a meeting for the high school students at the chapel. It was a busy life. The ladies at the chapel had a baby shower for Marie on January 17th and she received many lovely gifts.

I began working on my thesis and chose the subject "New Testament Church Organization." I wanted to study the subject thoroughly and be convinced that my views were Scriptural. In the graduate school I was the only one meeting with the assembly. All of the other men and women were in traditional churches. I remembered my experience in high school during the parade when I was the only one out of step! Could it be that I was out of step on my views now? But the more I studied, the more convinced I became. Scholars of every persuasion acknowledged that the early churches were led by elders, not by a clergyman, a pastor. My convictions were strengthened.

Mr. Maurice Martin, a Christian at Bethany who laid carpet, gave us a long runner of lovely rose carpet for the trailer. Marie wrote, "Makes the floor much warmer, makes the trailer look longer, more elegant!" The Christians at Wheaton were so very kind to us.

Monday, February 7th at 3:00 a.m. Marie's water broke and labor commenced. We drove to Geneva to the hospital at 7:00 a.m.. All day long she was in the labor room and then finally around 6 a.m., labor became more intense and the baby came at 2:15 a.m. the next morning. We had a little, healthy girl, 7lb. 3 oz. That was a long night but God had given us our first child and we were most grateful. I left at 3:15 a.m. and finally got to bed at 5:00 a.m. After Marie saw the baby she said, "Looks like Don and his mother!" Finally on February 16th they allowed Marie and the baby to come home. Our doctor was old fashioned and kept his patients in the hospital a long time. It was good to be together as a family and to adjust to having a baby. There was the wonder of new life; we consecrated her to God. We named her Donna Marie after both of us.

February 27th I was able to locate and rent a hall for the meetings in Warrenville Illinois. We had been meeting in a home but it became too crowded. We were trusting the Lord to cause the work to flourish. March 5th at an Emmaus meeting in Chicago with Ed Harlow, Bill MacDonald and Ben Tuininga, it was decided that we would go to Toronto to help with the work there in the fall. Marie and I had peace about this decision. The rest of the spring was busy with classes, writing my thesis and working as an assistant to one of the professors. It was perhaps the busiest year of our life.

This next year of our life will have to come from memory. The diary has been lost. That spring was very busy. I finished my thesis and required course work. Dr. Merril Tenney was my advisor and was very kind and helpful. He was urging me to go on for my Ph D in the fall but our course was set to teach at Emmaus. My thesis committee drilled me at my oral exam, seeking to point out flaws in my argument. Then I was sent to an adjoining room while they discussed it. One man in particular was hostile, —not wanting to pass me, on the work. But I heard Dr. Tenney say, "We may not agree on some of his conclusions, but it is a good piece of work and we should pass it." I heaved a sigh of relief when they brought me word.

I went to one more session of summer school to finish my undergraduate requirements. I took the book of Romans with Kenneth Kantzer. After this we took off to California on a quick trip to see family before moving to Canada. Marie's parents were delighted to see Donna Marie, their first granddaughter. Then it was back to Wheaton to sell our trailer and load up our belongings before heading for Toronto. I received my M. A. degree at the end of summer, very grateful for the helpful studies I had taken. The assembly in Wheaton was glad to give us a letter of commendation to the Lord's work and we began a life of faith, depending on the Lord to supply all our needs. While in school we had the GI Bill to pay for my education but now that was all over. It was an exciting step and we had some apprehensions but we believed God could supply. Elisha cried as he began his ministry after Elijah was taken from him, "Where is the Lord God of Elijah?" With Elisha, we believed the God who provided for Elijah was still able to provide food and shelter for His servants today.

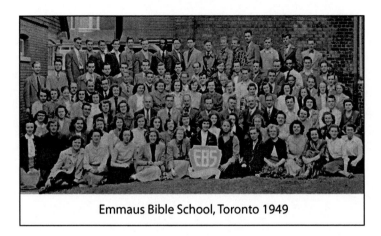

Emmaus Bible School, Toronto 1949

8

EMMAUS BIBLE SCHOOL

As we entered Canada we became aware that we were in another country. We were driving on the King's Highway toward Toronto. A sign said, "Treat our American tourists well. We need American dollars." In Toronto we were warmly welcomed by the staff and students. They helped us locate an apartment and get settled. We rented from the Waymans and had a comfortable basement apartment fairly close to the Harlows. Ed would pick me up in the morning for school and Marie would baby-sit for them at times so Margaret, his wife, could be free.

There was a core group of teachers who taught through the year: Ed Harlow, John Smart, Ernest Tatham (founders of the school), Dudley Sherwood, Sydney Hoffman and myself. Then we had visiting instructors who would come for a month or so. A.P. Gibbs, George Landis, Peter Pell, Harold Harper and others took these special courses. There was a happy spirit of camaraderie and we had an excellent student body of about 150. Most were older and many had just been discharged from the service. Some came for one year; others stayed for the three years. I was to teach 2nd and 3rd year Greek, Bible Introduction, Remedial English and 1 and 2 Timothy. And I may have forgotten some other courses.

I was fresh out of graduate school and a disciplined student. Because of this, I am afraid I worked the students a little hard, but I loved teaching and the students seemed to enjoy the classes. After 54 years I am still in touch with some of those students and it is a joy to see most of them going on for the Lord. Many were from Canada but a number were from the United States. Some have spent their lives on foreign fields; others have been active here at home, some in full time work. To keep my Hebrew up, Ed Harlow and I read together each week.

Financially things were tight at first. I was unknown to assemblies in Canada and in October we were often down to almost nothing. Our income for October was $97.50. Rent took much of that and our food bill was around $35.00. Bread cost eleven cents and a quart of milk about the same. I was willing to get some part time work but my visa did not permit this. It was a good initiation into the life of faith and brought us often to our knees. But as the year went on the income increased. We never went hungry and we were used to economizing. We discovered the promise is true: *"My God shall supply all your need according to His riches in glory by Christ Jesus"* (Phil. 4:19). I did some speaking in the various assemblies around Toronto, although we made Gilead our home fellowship. We can only thank God for His goodness to us that first year. Our daughter Donna was growing and healthy. She brought us much joy.

Over Christmas we made a trip down to Mansfield, Ohio, and spent several days with Evan and Joan Adams at her mother's home. Evan was Marie's brother, and I performed their wedding in 1947, my first! It was a delightful, snowy Christmas. Then we drove over to Wheaton for a short visit with friends there. We drove back to Toronto, rested and ready for the spring semester. Classes were going well and I was enjoying the fellowship with the other teachers. They were dear, godly men. Ernie Tatham felt very strongly about prophecy, an area where I was more tolerant. But I felt very strongly about the New Testament pattern for the church, an area where he hung loose. We had some animated discussions about these matters! All of these men, I believe, are gone now, also Ed Harlow who was promoted to glory March 10, 2003, 5 days before his 95th birthday. They were devoted men and an encouragement to me.

I spoke at various assemblies in the area. I especially remember going to Hawksville and having dinner with the John

Martin family. They had a large family and I believe they had just had their eighth child. Mrs. Martin marveled that we had only one. She asked my wife, " What do you do with all of your time?" Marie thought she was busy with one child! It was an Amish community and the roads were filled with horses pulling wagons and buggies. John and his wife led many of them to the Lord. I also had some meetings in the Buffalo and Detroit areas, where I sold our car that was giving us trouble and bought a Ford from a Christian dealer.

The Chicago school was going well and it was decided that we should move to Chicago to help with the work there. The Tuiningas were going to be gone for the summer and they invited us to stay in their apartment, which was near the school. We moved when the semester was over, saying goodbye to many dear friends in Canada, but a little glad to be back in the States. We would have to adjust to apartment living in a big city. Later that summer we were able to get an apartment near the school, which was at 69th and Normal Streets. It was in the same building where Bill MacDonald lived, my old friend from Navy days. Marie was pregnant now with our second child, due in October. She was always a hard worker and canned tomatoes and peaches that summer to be enjoyed during the cold winter months. August 3rd, I was asked to perform the wedding of Dan and Evelyn Girdner at Fernwood Chapel. Both lived godly, faithful lives and are now at home with the Lord.

We decided to make the assembly at Washington Heights our home assembly and the Christians were delighted to have us. Don Hall was one of the elders there and he and I would often visit families together. He had a real shepherd's heart. That August I also had some meetings in Peoria, Illinois, with an assembly that met in a home. Don Taylor introduced me to them. I really loved helping those small groups. We saw some encouragement but the assembly lacked good stable families and did not flourish. While there Mr. LeTourneau invited me to speak to the workers at his large plant. Employees were invited to come to hear the gospel. He was a godly man, very generous toward the Lord's work. And he was an engineering genius, inventing many of the massive, earth moving machines that one sees today. He showed me around the plant and some of his newest inventions.

With September came school in a new location and a new student body. We lived only a block from school at 69th and Normal streets, so I could easily walk. I settled into my new schedule with enthusiasm. I was asked to handle the new gospel correspondence course and also handle some room rentals to students, besides my regular classes. Charles Van Ryn and I shared an office. Charles was a bluntHollander; you never needed to wonder what Charlie was thinking. He would tell you.He had gone to Dallas Seminary and he and I had some stimulating theological discussions, not always agreeing but always ending up friends. Again I carried a full load of subjects. The Chicago school was just beginning to expand to a three year school. The student body was somewhat younger; we were now getting more young people just out of high school, but as a whole they were serious and diligent students. I am still in touch with some of those former students, and have lots of good memories.

Marie loved to entertain guests and we often had faculty and students over for a meal. September 29th she noted that we had Ed Harlow and Gordon Mitchell from Toronto, Bill MacDonald, Ben Tuininga and Charles Van Ryn over for the evening meal. And her meals were always delicious. October 1st we had Bob and Marjorie Clingan over with their daughter Beth Ann for a meal. Bob was a student in Toronto and then came down to the Chicago school. They have been our dear friends since then and have served the Lord in Mexico for over fifty years. The women at our assembly had a baby shower for Marie in October and gave her a cash gift of $105.00. She said, "How good the Lord is!" That was a lot of money then.

The school had street meetings on Halstead St. and I enjoyed helping with those. There is no excitement like preaching the gospel to the lost and seeing the Holy Spirit at work. We continued having men over for a meal, especially the visiting staff, men like Harold Harper and George Landis, a former Baptist pastor. Marie would often take Donna for a walk in a city park nearby and I would join them when I could. Life in an apartment building can be confining.

Sunday, October 22nd, I spoke at the Laflin St. assembly. The next morning about 2:00 a.m. labor started for Marie and at 4:00 a.m. Bill MacDonald came to our apartment to care for Donna while we went to the hospital. Labor moved along more quickly this time and Dorothy Ellen was born at 9:22 a.m. God had given us a beautiful little girl. I brought them home on October 28th. Marie wrote that I carried them both up the stairs to our apartment! I was younger and stronger then. Our hospital bill was $84.00 and the doctor was $70.00 and all bills were paid. Marie wrote, "How wonderfully the Lord provides!"

November 1st, five were baptized at the Fernwood Chapel and I was asked to baptize them, my first baptism. On November 9th there was a Workers and Elders Conference at Champaign, Illinois, and I drove down with Ben Tuininga and Charles Van Ryn. They asked me to give a little report about the school. I did not get back to one of those conferences for ten years. It was good to see T.B. Gilbert there; he had been active in starting these conferences some years before. Ah, the joys of family life! Marie wrote: Very hectic day! Donna into everything. Got Mecca ointment & smeared it over her face and sleepers. Got honey bowl & feasted. While mommy talked to daddy on the telephone she found the cottage cheese carton and stuffed it down fist by fist. Later, Donna ran wild and ransacked the house, dragged clothing, baby blankets around and dumped them. This was while Marie was doing laundry in another room.

Looking back at Marie's diaries of those days I am amazed at the number of people we had over for meals. There were often groups of seven to ten students at our home, enjoying Christian fellowship and my wife's good cooking. For Christmas, 1950 Bill MacDonald had us over for a delicious dinner and then Bill came over to our apartment for the evening. Bill was often in our apartment. At the end of the year Marie totaled up our income: $2,471.37 with all bills paid. The Lord has taken good care of us.

The second semester we had a few new students with a total of 55. That spring I taught I Timothy at night school. Marie wrote of our new daughter, "Everyone agrees she's a good and a beautiful baby." We were enjoying our children. January 28th we had nine students over for dinner, among them Ted Carlson, who spent most of his life in Japan as a missionary and finally died from cancer. Ted was a gentle, sensitive soul. We had the Don DeWeeses in our home often too and they went on to serve the Lord in Brazil. Marie noted that on May 21st Don and Marian Herrington were married and I spoke at the reception. They have gone on faithfully for the Lord and been our friends through the years. School was finally over and the students scattered for the summer.

In June I was busy fixing up the school apartments for the next year students. We also made a trip to Grand Rapids, Michigan, to spend time with the Ken Ruiters and the assembly there. Ken and I were in the Navy together in San Diego. We also went up to Cadillac, Michigan to have meetings with a small assembly there. Then I spoke in Holland, Kalamazoo and Muskegon and showed some pictures of the school. We were trying to make the school better known. June 23rd I went to Lake Geneva for a youth camp, sharing the speaking with Harold Harper. It was my first Christian camp experience but it would not be my last.

The school wanted me to take a trip down into the South to inform assemblies of the work of the school. Tuesday, July 3rd, Dick Farstad, who was a student, and I left for a trip of two weeks. I soon discovered that I had forgotten my ties and Dick was kind enough to loan me his for the speaking engagements. We made a swing through South and North Carolina, visiting the various assemblies in the area and telling them of the school. We also visited the Blue Ridge Conference and met Mr. Frederick Tatford, a gifted Bible teacher from England, who was very appreciative of my thesis. *New Testament Church Organization* was first published in 1950 and has gone through several editions since. I am so thankful that the Lord has been able to use it. We finally arrived home on July 18th after a long, hard drive from Roanoke, Virginia.

Later that summer we made a trip to California to visit family, showing Emmaus slides in various cities along the way, St. Louis, Oklahoma City, Albuquerque and Tucson, where we stayed with the Lloyd Donaldsons, dear friends in the assembly. We visited my mother's grave and ordered a marker for it inscribed with her name and the words "For me to live–Christ." Surely that was true of her life. Then we drove around to revisit my old schools and see friends, introducing my little family. A lovely visit. We decided to drive across the desert at night and left at 7:00 p.m. on August 1 for Marie's folks in Rosemead. It was a long night and we finally arrived at 7:00 a.m. the next day.

It was a delightful visit with Marie's family and I spoke at a number of assemblies in the Los Angeles area. We were able to spend some time at the beach, enjoying the sea that I miss so much in the Midwest. I also was able to revisit San Diego and the Christians at Marlborough Street who were so kind to me during my Navy days. We then drove on to Santa Barbara to see our many friends there and stayed in our old apartment at the Reynolds. We again visited the beach and Marie wrote, "Donna was wild about the ocean!" The school was anxious for me to tell the various assemblies about Emmaus so we also had meetings in Atascadero and the Oakland area. It was a joy to see many friends, some of whom had been in our wedding, and the McKeones and Signe, who had been so kind to me during my Navy days.

We finally headed east with stops in Sacramento and Salt Lake City, again telling of the school and its work. The assembly in Salt Lake was small but had a nice building where we stayed. The Walter Simpsons were pillars in the work there. It is sad that in later years the work died out. We left Salt Lake and went to Steamboat Springs and stayed in a motel ($6.00). Marie said it was nice but expensive! Then it was on to Colorado Springs, where we stayed in the Childrens' Home, which was a vision of the John Waldens. It was a faith work, inspired by the work of George Mueller in England. The Waldens' son, Johnny, decided to come to Emmaus in the fall, the fruit of our visit. From there we went east to Wichita Kansas for a visit with the Herb Banks family, friends from college days. We finally arrived home in Chicago on September 1st, very weary. It makes me tired thinking of all the traveling we did that summer!

We had been living in a small one bedroom apartment; now a large five room apartment in the same building became available. Marie wrote, "Rather overwhelmed by space! Loveliest home the Norbies have ever had." Then we had a cleaning day for the third floor at the school, getting ready for classes. Afterwards the whole group came to our new apartment for refreshments, 23 in all. Marie was delighted to have more room. School registration began on September 11. On the 14th we had a campfire on the 55th St. Promontory, a city park, with 42 students. Marie wrote: "A lovely, calm, balmy evening with a full Harvest Moon shining on Lake Michigan. The loveliest night we have every seen in Chicago. Had songs, testimonies, etc." Good memories.

It was good to be back teaching classes and busy in the work. On September 14th we entertained Ken and Elaine Brooks, students we had known in Toronto, now on their way to the Philippines, along with the Ruddocks, missionaries to Honduras. Fred and Hilda Munnings stopped by on their way to India. Night school started and I taught a course, "How to Study the Bible." And Marie was constantly entertaining staff, students and other Christians. In November Bill MacDonald and I took the train to Toronto for a staff conference, a profitable time.

Thanksgiving Day that year was a happy time. We had six students over for a delicious dinner and fellowship. Marie wrote: "Thanksgiving Day 1951 and so much both materially and spiritually for the Norbies to give thanks for." Yes, the Lord had been good. That Saturday was the annual conference in Chicago and we went to hear James Gunn and Richard Hill.

About that time Marie began to suspect she was pregnant again and morning sickness began to set in. We were going to have another child, due in July.

Christmas eve we had our family time and Christmas day we had four students at noon for dinner and then a buffet for a larger crowd in the evening. Marie provided the main course but others contributed other dishes. It was a great evening of fellowship. I finished the year speaking at Knox, Indiana, taking Dick Farstad along. This was an assembly Mr. Gilbert had started years before. Friday, January 4th, we had a Western party with 29 present with all wearing jeans. We had two teams for games, the Cowboys and the Indians. I am sure we had some Scripture but I can't remember the passage. Maybe it was from Joshua with his conquest of the land!

About this time Marie wrote: "Time of much exercise of heart about severing connections with Emmaus." This is all she wrote but I know I was feeling restless. I loved the teaching and the atmosphere of study and preparation. The students were dear to our hearts and I loved the other teachers. So why would we even consider leaving such a ministry?

Perhaps it was too comfortable, too secure. We had read books on the lives of Anthony Norris Groves and George Mueller. At the school we felt the protection of an institution where giving was more sure. The staff was expected to speak at various assemblies in the area so I was rarely home on Sunday. This really was not good for those churches; they came to depend too much on Emmaus teachers. When Emmaus moved later, the local men had not developed their preaching and teaching gifts. Their tendency then was to hire a preacher. And I wanted to be more involved in evangelism, in seeing souls saved and then discipled; to see assemblies begun.

George Lang in England was a friend who encouraged me to think in these terms also.

During this time there was also opportunity to do some speaking on WMBI, the Moody station. One evening during January we had the Charles Van Ryns, Bill MacDonald, Ben Tuininga and Mr. Horton from Africa over for dinner. It was exciting to hear of his teaching and translation work in Africa. New Testament principles for the Lord's work are still effective. At this time too I was asked to write a correspondence course on Bible Study Methods, which Marie typed for me.

January 23rd Marie wrote, "Still praying daily about the move we should make, still much exercised about changing." January 31st she wrote, "Exercise of heart continues. Plan now to announce our resignation soon, in view of next year's plans being made now." February 3 she wrote, "Dittoed our statement of resignation and reasons, to be given to staff and others today. We wonder what the coming weeks hold. No leading as yet from the Lord as to where we should go from here. Oklahoma City on our minds still for some reason." But when we handed out the statement to the staff Bill wanted to talk with me. Marie wrote, "Talked situation over with Don, asked what his grievances were, what concessions can be made, etc. Assured Bill there is nothing personal behind our decision." Bill then talked a little about our differences on eschatology; he is more dogmatic than I am. For some, details of prophecy are a touchstone of orthodoxy. So, the die was cast. May the Lord guide us.

We were still buying cars. We always bought used cars and put a lot of mileage on them. This meant they needed replacing periodically. So in February we bought a 1950 Studebaker Champion, dark green in color. Marie wrote, "Our daddy is pleased with it." I continued to be busy with meetings in the various assemblies as well as classes at school. Don Hall and I did a lot of visitation together; Don was a dear man with a gentle, shepherd's heart. Marie's check up revealed a chronic bronchitis. The doctor said to watch it, or move to Arizona! Maybe it was another reason to leave the Chicago area.

David Kirk, an Irish evangelist, had some meetings in Chicago and it was good to see him again. I still remember a message he gave in Toronto on John the Baptist, a man sent from God. Clark McClelland was having meetings with him and we had them over for supper. Marie wrote of David, "interesting and vivacious!" Leonard Lindsted, from Wichita, and Tom McCullagh, who lived in Oklahoma, also had meetings in the area about this time. We had them over for a meal and they urged us to consider moving to Oklahoma and mentioned Tulsa as a needy city. When the word spread that we would be leaving Emmaus, the folk at Washington Heights and our other Chicago friends expressed deep disappointment. We had become very close to many Christians there.

Thursday, April 10th, I caught a train to Wichita and then went down to Tulsa with Leonard Lindsted, who was especially interested in seeing us move there. Several families met in a home and we had a meeting with them that night. They were encouraging us to move there. The next day we went to Oklahoma City for their conference on Saturday. Leonard also wanted me to look at Topeka, so we went up there early Sunday and met the Christians there. Florence Thomas, an Emmaus student who was there, wanted me to visit Lawrence and we rode the bus over there for the evening meeting. We had supper at Bill Sommerville's home and I spoke at the evening meeting. After the meeting I caught a train for Kansas City and Chicago, arriving home about 10 a.m. What a hectic weekend! But Leonard wanted me to see the various possibilities. There was much to pray about.

During April I went down to Knox, Indiana, for a Sunday and took Hassell Mayberry and his young wife along. Hassell at that time was a promising student, showing spiritual leadership. The sad ending is that when he left Emmaus he went to University and lost his faith. He has since died and never came back to God. It makes me weep to think of Hassell.

Marie was beginning to pack and get ready for a move. May 2nd Washington Heights had a farewell meal for us. Marie wrote,"Some nice things said about the Norbies." They gave us a gift of $100.00. They were very kind to us.

Beginning May 5th I gave my final exams to students, feeling a tinge of sorrow that this would be my last time with them. We had come to love those students very dearly. And Thursday, May 8th they had a lovely banquet for us at the school. All the board and staff were there. There were skits and readings by students and a final message by John Walden, Sr.,on Ezekiel, but I do not remember the content! They gave me a beautiful briefcase and stainless steel table ware for the family. Marie wrote, "The Norbies were touched and appreciative–and amazed at such a send off. A very happy and memorable evening."

Students helped me load a trailer and we shipped some things. We had decided to go to Tulsa and try to help the little work there. On May 12 I left for Tulsa pulling the trailer. Marie and the children left the next day by train. Ben Tuininga took them to the station and was very helpful. Our girls were all excited about traveling on a train! There was no food available except in the diner. So Marie wrote, "Had a delicious supper for $1.99, for the three children behaved perfectly." Prices have surely gone up since then! They arrived at 10:15 p.m. that night and I had arrived earlier and was able to meet them. It was a happy reunion. This would be a new chapter in our lives. Now we were away from the comfort zone of the school but we believed that the God who had supplied all of our needs for the past three years could continue to supply them (Phil. 4:19).

9

OKLAHOMA, THE SOONER STATE

We arrived in Tulsa full of zeal and enthusiasm for the work. But first I needed to find a place to live. We stayed temporarily with the Cox family. I located an apartment in a Veteran's housing project, four rooms for $40.00 a month. It would give us temporary housing while I looked for a house.

Within a week we were able to move into our apartment, which was spartan at best. We had been spoiled by that nice apartment in Chicago.

I was house hunting, reading the classified ads, wondering if we could find a house we could afford to buy.

We finally found an older house at 2604 E. 10th Street that we thought we could afford and put in a bid on it. We prayed for the Lord's will to be done. Our bid was accepted; the deal was closed and we were busy buying used furniture and cleaning up the house. It was in desperate need of painting so I worked hard to get it painted before we moved in. We were anxious to get settled because we expected our third child about the first of July. Marie was uncomplaining and a hard worker as we readied the house so we could move in.

Bill Paterson, a gifted evangelist, was having meetings in Oklahoma City and came up on June 11 to encourage us. We had a picnic lunch with him in the park, much cooler than in our apartment. June 13 we finally moved into our "new" house; our first. The heat of an Oklahoma summer had set in and

Marie was very glad to be out of that little, stifling apartment.

There were a few older people in the meeting and one younger family, the Noel Gardners. Noel was a big native American from southern Oklahoma who had been saved out of a rough, drunken life, resulting in a prominent scar across his face. He and I became close friends. Noel loved the Lord and was zealous in sharing the gospel.

Noel had a P.A. system and loved to do street work. We would drive to Collinsville, a little town near Tulsa, put the speakers on the roof of his car and preach the gospel. Then we would talk to people who came by and hand out tracts. We also had meetings in Broken Bow.

Unfortunately our experience with the little meeting was not encouraging. Noel and I were zealous in the gospel but some older believers were content to stay as a small home meeting, breaking bread and doing little more. Marie wrote on June 15th, "begins to look like the Norbies had better not plan on a stay in Tulsa. He could do no mighty works because of their unbelief." It was disheartening; what should we do?

On Wednesday, June 25th, I spoke on 2 Chronicles 7:14 and emphasized the need to humble ourselves and to pray for the Lord's blessing. The prayers that followed were self righteous, and complacent: "we are God's people, standing for the truth, keeping His testimony pure, this is a day of small things, etc." After the meeting the older men spoke very harshly to me and we realized it would not be possible for us to work with them. Noel Gardner was very upset and wanted us to start another meeting with him. But we had no peace about that and decided we would need to move.

The assembly on the south side of Oklahoma City had urged us to consider moving there. I drove down to talk to the elders there and was encouraged. They spoke of their concern to see a work start on the north side of their great, sprawling city. They would be delighted if we would move there and begin a work. I returned home to discover the baby was ready to come. Tuesday, July 1st our first son was born, a big, healthy boy. I greeted Marie with the words, "It's a boy!" We named him Daniel Eric, trusting he would become a man of God like Daniel. I took them home on July 4th; both were doing well.

Leonard Lindsted wanted us to look at Topeka for a possible move. I drove to Wichita on July 9th and we drove up to Topeka. But we did not have peace about moving there. It was a small, struggling assembly at that time. Richard Burson from Hutchinson, Kansas, was having Daily Vacation Bible School in Oklahoma City and I drove down to visit him and to look at houses there. Richard and I began a friendship that was to last for many years.

We put the house on the market and prayed about the sale of it. Our painting and cleaning of the house paid off. The realtor who sold us the house brought a buyer by to see it. They liked it and bought it for $7,200.00 which was $400.00 more than we paid for it. We saw the Lord's hand opening the way for us to move. Marie wrote, "Seems too good to be true." Our experience in Tulsa was very trying for her. The weather was hot, 102 humid degrees, a typical Oklahoma summer. We found a home at 2004 North Eastern in Oklahoma City that would meet our needs and were able to buy it. August 7th we moved from Tulsa and settled in to our new home. Tulsa is a beautiful city but our experience there was not pleasant. Marie was a dear, patient wife through it all. The Oklahoma City Christians were very warm in welcoming us to their city.

Ben Parmer, a wheat farmer from Burlington, Colorado, was going to have tent meetings in Henryetta and invited me to help. We left on August 9th in his pick-up with the tent. Marie was busy getting settled in her new home. Ben had done tent work before and I was the novice. With the help of local men we erected the tent on a vacant lot and tied into electricity from a neighbor. The next day, Sunday, we began our meetings in the evening. The fellowship there was a small home meeting and certainly needed help. We rented a room in a cheap motel and ate some of the meals with the Christians. It was miserably hot, up to 110 degrees, but we persevered, every morning going door to door with tracts and invitations. Ben was a hard worker with a passion for evangelism.

Tent work can be exciting; it is like fishing in a new lake. One is never sure how many will come and what the response will be. We would open the meetings with the singing of some rousing, gospel songs and then both of us would speak for about 30 minutes each. Ben had put up a Two Roads chart which he liked to use. It made people aware visually of the need to get saved. At first we had quite a number of Pentecostals that came. They wanted us to speak on the Holy Spirit but when we did they were not pleased and quit coming. They believed in the "baptism" with the speaking in tongues and felt we were not very spiritual.

One night an older man was going out of the tent and I stopped him and asked, "What are you trusting to get you to heaven?" He stood straight and tall, looked me in the eye and said, "My good life!" Later in the meetings he wanted to talk to us and confessed he had lived a wicked life and needed to be saved. That night he professed to turn to Christ. He was 71 years old but said he had never heard the gospel before. A young girl also professed Christ. But we did not have too much response from the meetings. Marie wrote that the children were well and that Danny was growing. She also wrote, "The Lord met our need today and brought in $69.40 in four different gifts!" I am so grateful that throughout our married life she has never complained about finances, a real woman of faith.

After two weeks we concluded the meetings and took down the tent. Ben had heard of a small home meeting in Rogers, Arkansas, and wanted to visit them. We drove over and met the folks and had a few meetings before driving home. We bought two baskets of Arkansas peaches for canning and arrived home on Thursday, the 27th, very weary. The Guthrie assembly had purchased an old church building and refurbished it. They were having an opening conference that weekend and Ben wanted to stay for it before going home. Tom McCullagh had seen that work begin with tent meetings some years before. Leonard, Ben and I were involved in the speaking. It was a happy, profitable time. It was my joy to be with them fifty years later for their anniversary!

I was concerned to try another series of tent meetings near Oklahoma City before cold weather set in. Ben said he would help if I could get a lot for the tent. I looked around and found a lot that we could use in Dell City, a suburb. Saturday, September 7th, we put up the tent with men from the assembly helping and started the meetings the next night. The Christians came out well and some unsaved were coming. We worked the neighborhood with invitation and tracts. That Saturday we went to Guthrie to help with their street meeting. Some nights cars would stop near the tent to listen. The next Tuesday, after the meeting, Ray Mangum was weeping. His wife was a believer and he had come to realize his terrible, lost condition. With tears that night he professed Christ. In the days that followed he went on well for the Lord. Some others also professed Christ. Howard Kirksey was one of these, now at home with the Lord.

Ben had to leave on Friday for a conference in Colorado and I concluded the meetings on Sunday night. Monday, September 22nd, we took the tent down and on Tuesday Donna went with me as I took the tent to Wichita to return it to Leonard, who owned it. We used a truck belonging to one of the Christians. We also visited our friends, the Banks, in Wichita before returning home.

I had been away so much but now it was time to work on the house, painting and repairing. There were opportunities to speak at Guthrie and Oklahoma City. Tom McCullagh was a fervent, gospel preacher. He once said in a meeting, "Now Norbie is a teacher; I am not." So Guthrie was glad to get some teaching of the Word.

The Christians of the area assemblies had a surprise house warming for us the last of September, bringing us piles of food, cases of canned goods, 50lb. of potatoes, etc. It was a very loving, warm reception. We felt very welcomed to Oklahoma City. Marie and I had a real concern for the young people and had them over for a party. Eighteen came from Guthrie and Oklahoma City. This was the beginning of an extensive work with the young people. Marie began a girls' Bible club that she conducted for years. Women who were in her club fifty years ago still have good memories of those times. One told me, "We always felt Mrs. Norbie was a model mother and wife, a pattern for us to follow."

We often entertained guests and service men would frequently come up for the weekend. David Joye, Ben Earthman, Maurice Martin and Jerry Keller were among these. Our dear friends, the Bob Clingans, came and stayed with us for several days in October on their way to Mexico to serve the Lord. Our children enjoyed their Beth Ann and Darrell. The last of October I went to Rogers for two weeks of meetings with the little group there. While doing door to door work I was confronted by a Baptist preacher who wanted me to leave town; he said my message was false and my baptism was "alien baptism." It is good to know the call of God at times like that. A couple of young people professed Christ during the meetings.

Bill Sommerville from Lawrence and Richard Burson from Hutchinson came down on December 9 for a few days of prayer and fellowship. Richard had been encouraging me to help with the work of Kansas Bible Camp next year. Both men had a deep concern and love for young people. Then on the 14th the Tuiningas came through on their way to Mexico with Tom Sands, a missionary from Uruguay and stayed with us. It was good to see them again and to hear news of Emmaus.

It had been a busy, eventful year for the Norbies. Of Christmas eve Marie wrote, "Had our traditional oyster stew and then started our Christmas. Read story of our Lord's birth and sang, etc. Began opening packages." And then she listed the presents we all received. Surely the Lord had taken good care of us through the year. He had provided us a home and we had all our bills paid. Our hearts were filled with love for Him and one another. Christmas day we had guests for dinner, among them Jerry Keller, a service man from St. Louis.

We were interested in starting a Missionary Study Class for the area and had our first meeting on January 6 with the Tuiningas and Tom Sands on their return from Mexico. Tom spoke of the work in Uruguay and they told of their trip to Mexico. Some letters from missionaries were read and there was a good time of prayer. We wanted to see the Christians informed and praying for the Lord's work in other areas. It was a good beginning.

I tried going over to Rogers a number of times that winter but lacked a solid core group with which to work. One family that had shown interest was moving. I finally decided I needed to put in my time elsewhere. I would spend more time in Oklahoma City and Guthrie, seeking to build the work there. On February 11th, a Wednesday, we had Frank and Barbara Moffitt with their son Philip over for a meal. They had been in a Baptist church but were interested in the assembly. Frank was a geologist with Texaco and had been transferred to Oklahoma City. It was the beginning of a long, happy friendship and they came into the assembly, having become convinced of New Testament principles for the church.

Funds had been a little low but Marie wrote that $75.00 came in "so mama went shopping for needed groceries." Lean times would come to test and toughen our faith and then the Lord would provide. I had told the Lord I was willing to take employment if necessary but he always provided just what we needed. Marie was a frugal shopper and she always canned fruit for the winter. We would buy in quantity, such as dried milk, 100 lbs. for $18.00. The doctor assured us it was just as nourishing as the whole milk for the children and we drank a lot of it as our family grew. The spring of 1953 I planted a garden, which was a real help in supplementing our diet. This became an annual event and we also planted fruit trees wherever we lived.

Days were busy with meetings and visitation. We had some cottage meetings in Shawnee and Ponca City. I bought a P.A. system and we had street meetings in various towns around. In May I visited Bob Gritman, a former Emmaus student, at Fort Smith, Arkansas. Bob was in training in the army and he was upset over the bayonet drill they were having. Soldiers back from Korea were training them to kill ruthlessly. Bob was upset and said, "Don, I don't know if I can kill a man!" We talked and prayed and I told him to talk to his commanding officer about his feelings. But it is best to express such reservations when one first goes in. It is a dilemma for a Christian in the armed forces.

We were involved in several conferences during May 1953. On the 16th we were in Wichita for their spring conference. The next weekend was the Oklahoma City conference. Leonard Lindsted, Tom McCullagh, John McGeehee from Memphis and I spoke. John told of his experiences as a prisoner of the communists in China, a moving account. Then the following weekend we were off to Memphis for meetings. We stayed with the McGeehees in their lovely apartment over the chapel in a large, old southern mansion. They told us of the struggles of the work there. Then it was home to Oklahoma City. That was a busy month! Conferences can be encouraging times of hearing the Word, prayer and fellowship, deepening the spiritual bonds between believers.

In July we took a family trip south to Turner Falls and Platt National Park. It was a happy time with the children enjoying playing in the water. Marie wrote, "Finally home about 7:00 dirty & tired." Danny was growing well and beginning to walk, a big accomplishment in a young life.

July 5th Tom started tent meetings in Guthrie and asked me to help. The tent was erected on the west side of Guthrie and we worked the area with tracts and invitations. It was hot work. On July 8th we had a violent, thunder storm that threatened to blow the tent away. Some took the children to the cars while others hung on to the tent ropes and prayed. Tom would keep on preaching through it all. I spoke briefly at the end in a torrential downpour.

Following this I went to Albuquerque for a series of meetings with the assembly. There was good interest and it was encouraging. Over the years I visited them periodically. I returned home on July 31st; Marie wrote, "One very tired Daddy tonight." But Tom wanted to start tent meetings in Edmond, a town ten miles north of Oklahoma City. He wanted me to help and we started meetings on August 2nd. We experienced opposition from the ministerial association. They said that Edmond had plenty of churches; that was true but often there was not a clear gospel presented. On August 11th we had another violent storm that threatened to uproot the tent. Torrential rain began as I was speaking. My wife wrote, "Don went ahead preaching through howling wind and crashing thunder. Had to shout to be heard and shouted himself almost hoarse. Tom didn't speak and had time of singing until storm abated. Very exciting." The tent meetings concluded but we continued to go to Edmond for street meetings.

On August 17 Kansas Bible Camp began for two weeks and Richard asked me to help with the teaching. I also was the counselor for some of the older boys. Two of my boys stole the water melon which was to be used for watermelon polo in the pool and hid it under my bunk. Then they accused me of the theft! For several years we rented the Salvation Army camp on the north side of Wichita for our camp. That year thirteen young people professed Christ, some from Oklahoma City. We would haul youngsters up from both Oklahoma City and Guthrie. Karl Pfaff, a preacher from Iowa, and I worked together for a number of years with Richard in the camp work.

Richard discovered a former country club for sale near Hutchinson. The camp made a bid on it and we were able to buy the property. We incorporated and began the extensive work of rejuvenating the place. What a mess! It had been used for cattle and the storage of hay and was in terrible disrepair. But Christians volunteered to clean up the place and camp began in 1956. Kansas Bible Camp has continued through the years and been a blessing to many young people. I am still on the board, the only one left of the original men who incorporated.

In September we made a quick trip to California to see relatives. We did some crazy things on trips like that, driving all night to make time and to save on motel bills. I wanted to revisit Prescott, my old childhood home. We drove south from Flagstaff to Prescott, saw our little house and my old school; good memories. Then it was on to California for a family visit. I spoke in several assemblies in the area and was able to visit the assembly in Santa Barbara and renew my love for the sea! Then it was back to Oklahoma, with a stop in Tucson on the way to see friends and speak at the meetings. I visited my mother's grave again, to thank God for her and to give myself afresh to the Lord. Dear Mother! I often wish my wife and children had known her.

10

A New Assembly

In October I spoke at the Elm Springs Conference, a country assembly in central Kansas. Good meetings and fellowship. Then it was home for the beginning of the new assembly on the north side of Oklahoma City. We had been having Bible studies with a view to the start of the work and on October 25, 1953, we began to break bread and to function as an assembly. We met in the Frank Moffitt home, the Moffitts, the Webbs, the Nelsons, Norbies and Royal Lockhart. Sunday school was held in the kitchen! It was a happy day filled with joy and the expectation of God's blessing.

The children were growing and doing well. Dr. Garrison was our doctor, a kindly, generous man. Those were the days when doctors gave a special rate to those in the Lord's work! Marie wrote concerning Danny, "Dr. says he is a fine specimen of humanity!" Sounds like a proud mother! We were thankful for healthy, growing children.

Starting an assembly is hard work, especially when the group is so small. I was constantly doing door to door work and visitation, besides the meetings. I was also helping with the other meeting in Oklahoma City and with Guthrie. Then there were times when I had meetings in other cities. There is always plenty to do in the Lord's work.

During November, William (Bill) Pell had a series of meetings at the south side assembly using his model of the tabernacle.

We attended those and had Bill over for a meal. We had visited the Pell family in Grand Rapids in years past, an amazing family dedicated to the work of the Lord. Bill's brother Peter was also a gifted preacher. Also during the month Donna seemed troubled about her "sins" and prayed. It was quite spontaneous on her part and marked the beginning of spiritual interest that was to continue.

That December we had to get a different car. Marie wrote that it was a 1952 Plymouth for $995.00 "and we had only $14 left to our name!" But we were used to living close to the edge. Also we had decided the assembly would be established on the west side of town and we should move to that area. We sold our house and bought one at 3136 N. W. 29th Street on December 14. It was a little smaller house but would serve our family for the present. And it was a much better location. We also discovered that month that we would be having another child. Well, the Lord said, "Be fruitful and multiply!" But it meant Marie would feel miserable for the first few months. We had a lovely Christmas with our traditional oyster stew on Christmas eve. 1953 was about over, a fruitful, busy year.

1954 started well with our move into our new house and getting settled. Marie wrote of "making curtains for our kitchen out of feed sacks." We had come to know the Herschel Martindale's and had Bible studies with them. Herschel was a student at the college in Edmond and became interested in Biblical principles for the church. They then started going to the assembly in Guthrie. It was the beginning of a long friendship; we worked together for years in camp work and also in gospel meetings. During February, I had a series of meetings in Albuquerque that were encouraging. Over the years I would have meetings over the Southwest in Lubbock, Albuquerque, Las Cruces, El Paso, Odessa, Waco, Houston and Dallas.

In April I had two weeks of meetings with the small assembly in Hutchinson and enjoyed time with the Bursons. Richard was building on his house and I helped some with that. I then drove over to the fellowship in Lawrence and had meetings with them. Bill Sommerville had a good work going with university students.

The meetings were moved from the Moffitt home to ours but we were cramped for room and were looking for a better meeting place. In May we were able to get the use of a union hall at 12th and May Streets for our Sunday meetings. This gave us plenty of room, although it was very crude. We often had to clean up the place for our meetings. We continued to have street meetings in Norman on Saturday nights. One evening, while we were speaking, a drunk came up and began to shout, "I believe in God. I believe in Jesus!" Like many others he had a religious experience to talk about but lacked evidence of repentance and a changed life.

That June we erected the tent on the west side of the city and had an evangelistic series. It was hot, 100 degrees plus, but I kept at the door to door work. James Nelson helped me with the speaking. We ran the series for three weeks and saw some strangers in but not the response we would have liked. We took the tent down on July 10. Most of the saints had been out faithfully, some every night.

That was a hot summer; July 11 it was 108 degrees. Marie said there were 35 consecutive days over 100. She was pregnant and the baby was due very soon. She was miserable in the heat but not a complainer. The okra in the garden did well; it likes the heat. The garden helped a lot; we ate okra every day. On July 21 Marie wrote, "Norbies passing through a time of slim finances. Don may have to work with his hands a while, as did Paul." July 27th she wrote: "Norbies in a very low financial state. $8 the in bank, very low income this month. Don thinking seriously of looking for employment. House payment to make, Doctor's and hospital to pay." Those times are not easy to endure but they do test your commitment and build faith.

On August 2 Marie wrote: "The Lord provided enough in fellowship yesterday to finish meeting the house payments and get a few groceries. He is good to His own." On August 5: "Some income has come this week, have decided to put off idea of finding employment 'til after baby & after camp." We also canned 19 quarts of peaches on that day. Finally on the 7th we went to the hospital around 11:00 a.m. and the baby was born at 12:35 p.m. We named him Dale Victor, after Marie's father. He was a big one, 9 lb. 5 oz. "Afterwards had a sweet time reading & praying with a sweet husband, then a quiet, relaxing afternoon."

We had been praying that we would have adequate funds to pay the hospital bill. We took mother and baby home on August 12. Marie wrote: "Once again we were able to meet the hospital bill on time, thanks to the Lord's timed provision. Adequate gifts came in yesterday to meet the need, most from folks who know nothing of our expected arrival. The Lord is very good to us in every way." Yes, Lord, You are good!

The latter part of August it was camp again at Kansas Bible Camp, hauling youngsters up from Oklahoma. It was a fruitful time; some accepted the Lord. When I was home there was always visitation and some were getting saved through the door-to-door work. Then there was the struggle to see them go on for the Lord. Hospital visitation also was profitable. Some were being saved and added to the church. September 19 we had 33 out to the meetings. Late in September I made a trip to Chicago, stayed with Bill MacDonald and spoke at meetings in the area. I also visited Grand Haven, Michigan and the Pells in Grand Rapids, Michigan before returning home.

In November I went to Albuquerque to help with the finishing of their new chapel. Then on November 21 the new chapel was opened and I had a series of meetings. It is a lovely building and fits into the decor of the Southwest. We prayed that the Lord would use it for His honor and glory. We closed the meetings on Dec. 2 and I drove to El Paso. One couple had professed to be saved. I only stayed overnight in El Paso with the Jim Hunts and drove on down to Chihuahua City and then west to the small town of General Trias, where the Clingans were living and serving God. We love the Clingans and it was a great time of meetings and village work. Bob was building a house for them and we worked together on it. I arrived home on the 13th, having driven all the way from El Paso, a long day. It was good to get home. Later I began having symptoms of amoebic dysentery and that troubled me for a number of years; I had picked it up in Mexico and it took many courses of treatment before it finally cleared up. I had some fierce bouts of diarrhea.

A NEW ASSEMBLY

Christmas that year saw several ill. Marie was very sick with a high fever and I had to cook the dinner. We were given a ham and had a good meal together. Marie was better by the end of the year. She wrote, "Have also reviewed the Lord's goodness to us financially in 1954; our income was $3216.44 ($2837.71 after travel expense was deducted.) "He crowneth the year with His goodness."

In January Marie had surgery for varicose veins and spent some days recuperating. On January 25, 1955, she wrote: "Special day here for prayer and reading the Word. We are giving serious thought to the feelings we've had since about late summer about going to Mexico. We are seeking to know the Lord's mind more fully and want to have hearts willing for anything He may indicate." But we felt the new assembly needed to be more established before considering leaving it. Also during this month Donna did make a clear profession of trusting Christ. Marie wrote that "she seems to be really trusting the Lord for salvation. She was eager to kneel and thank the Lord Jesus for saving her. So did Mother and Daddy." We never tried to push our children in this matter, realizing it must be a work of the Spirit of God if it is to be lasting.

March 1st we located a surplus government building for sale that had two four room apartments. The assembly decided to buy it and move it on a lot. We could remodel it for a small chapel, removing the walls of the one apartment for a meeting room. We located one lot for the chapel but the neighbors objected and the deal fell through. We did not want to take legal action. A Mr. Stone, who was one of the opposing neighbors, offered to loan us the money to buy a different lot! We located a lot on N. Portland, a better location, and purchased it. So all turned out well.

We had led a Mr. Sills to the Lord. He was a broken, older man. One leg had been amputated. He had been a hard man, cursing and abusing his wife, a rough old rancher. After he was saved he would often sit and weep as he thought of his past life. His wife was a sweet Christian and died that March. We had the funeral in Hennessey, Oklahoma, with a large crowd present. It was a great opportunity to preach the gospel.

In April we began digging the footing for the chapel, all with volunteer help. Royal was a plumber so he did our plumbing. When the foundation was laid we had the building moved in. We placed it far enough back on the lot so we could build on a larger chapel in the front. Some were being saved and baptized. Mrs. McComb was brightly saved and baptized. She wept at her baptism; her husband was too drunk to come. He died later in a car accident, driving drunk. We continued with street meetings in various towns and also had a radio broadcast for some time.

Marie noted a conference in Wichita on May 15 where several preachers were present. A Mr. John Ferguson from Detroit spoke and blasted the assembly movement as a failure. "Don rose to defend faithfulness to New Testament principles, said we can't condone our failures, but the pattern must be followed." I had forgotten it but that must have been a heavy session! I assured Mr. Ferguson that there was nothing personal in my comments. The conference ended on a good note.

Tuesday., June 7th, "Our 8th wedding anniversary. Celebrated it by buying ½ gal. ice cream to the delight of the children. Great splurge, as we have surely been low financially. But the Lord meets our needs just in time, just when groceries are all gone, etc. He has been very gracious to us these 8 years." Amen! Then Archie and Virginia Ross, missionaries from Africa, visited us and had a number of meetings. Dear people! Archie had been a friend since our Toronto days.

It was another hot summer and meetings in the union hall were very hot. With the other brothers I worked a lot on the building we had moved in to. We worked the whole building over and also put on a new roof. Hot work in the Oklahoma sun! The income was low and we decided to discontinue the radio broadcast. Marie wrote, "We are living almost entirely on vegetables from our garden: squash, greens, string beans, some carrots and turnips." The okra did well too. She also wrote, "Yet we find quietness of heart in circumstances that would upset most." I was also having a weekly Bible study in Blackwell and some were saved.

The union had allowed us the free use of their hall for eighteen months; the Lord's provision. But finally our building was finished and we had our first meeting on Sunday, October 23; our daughter Dorothy's birthday. Ben Parmer came for a series of gospel meetings beginning that day. Ben and I did extensive house to house work during the day. We did see a number of unsaved come and one night had 41 out, quite a crowd for our small building! The visitation did bring in strangers on the following Sundays. Maurice Martin called us to say he was stationed at Tinker Field and would like to come over. We had known Maurice as a high school boy in Wheaton and were glad to renew the friendship. He began coming to meetings and one night after prayer meeting he told us that he had received the Lord that night. He has gone on to live for the Lord. And so the Lord gave encouragement from time to time.

I was asked to visit a man in the Veteran's hospital who had a leg amputated and was very depressed. He was a truck driver and now could no longer drive. Through visits he came to know the Lord. While visiting him I met a man in the hall who was dying of bone cancer. His name was Buddy Martin and he was a very troubled man. He said to me that he was not ready to die; he knew he was a sinner. After several visits he accepted the Lord and became a bright witness for his Saviour. His wife, Chiquita also turned to the Lord. Buddy wanted to be baptized with his wife. I was rather fearful that he might break a bone during the baptism; his bones were so weak. But all went well and it was a time of rejoicing. Some months later Buddy died and I was with him the day he died. Buddy was loved by all. His doctor even donated blood to him and the hospital staff wept when he died. We had the funeral and at least two were saved as the gospel was preached. I know Buddy rejoiced.

In January 1956 we were moved deeply by the news of the five missionaries being killed by the Auca Indians in Ecuador. I knew three of them who were from assemblies and was close to Jim Elliott. He and I often communicated and I felt a special sense of loss. The Lord used their lives and deaths to challenge many to give their lives to God. In 1972 I was able to visit Arajuno, the base they left to contact the Waorani (Auca) Indians, a moving experience. It was a joy to see the assembly, begun by them, going on for the Lord.

LIFE IS A MOUNTAIN

In April 1956 I had meetings at the assembly in South Houston. Gospel meetings were preceded by a week of teaching meetings. There was good interest and the Lord blessed. A brother in the fellowship talked to me privately and said he was praying that his wife would get saved. He said, "She does not think she can be forgiven. One night after I had come home from the war she awakened me sobbing. She said she had lived with a man for six months while I was gone. It hurt me but I have forgiven her because I have come to know the Lord. Now I want to see her come to know forgiveness."

This spoke to my own heart and I felt deeply convicted. There were people I had not forgiven; one was my father. I remember going to my room that night and getting on my knees and crying out to God with tears for help to forgive some who had wronged me. I remember writing to my father and assuring him of my love and forgiveness. Some years later as he was facing surgery he finally turned to the Lord at age 70. I believe my forgiving him may have helped. From that time on we could pray together and I heard him often thank God for forgiveness. And the good news is that the man's wife professed Christ during those meetings.

I was learning to make car repairs too. Jim Nelson was a good mechanic and he would help me. One car we tore down the engine, thinking it just needed rings. It turned out the engine was in bad shape. We had to rebore the block and put in oversized pistons. The parts bill was much more than we counted on and we were short on funds. We ended up borrowing money from the children's piggy banks. I had a bag full of change as I paid the bill. The parts man laughed and said, "It looks like you robbed the kids' piggy banks!" I just smiled. Marie wrote, "Our finances are at an all time low with 1 cent in the bank account." But then the Lord provided once again.

The Clingans came through for a visit on their way back to Michigan. They were still urging us to move down that way so that we could work together more. We were very compatible in our views. We continued to pray about the possibility. The Bob Sawyers and the whole assembly in Albuquerque were urging us to move there; we also thought of El Paso. At this time I also began going to Ponca City for a weekly Bible study in the Secrests' home. Mrs. Secrests' husband, Bill, was not saved yet but was friendly. I also painted and fixed up our house so it would qualify for a loan if we put it on the market. Some were being saved and baptized through visitation and our meetings at the chapel.

August 13-17 we were at Kansas Bible Camp for our first grade school camp in the new facility. It was a hot week,105-110 degrees. The swimming pool was a popular place for campers then and it still is. I went back on the weekend and brought up another load of campers.

This was a Jr. High camp. One event was a Hobo Breakfast where campers cooked their own breakfast, bacon and eggs on a stove made of a gallon can. The kids loved it. This has become a camp tradition.

The following week was for those in high school and college. Camps were quite full; the Lord blessed and a number were saved. Mary from Oklahoma City brought her friend Jess and before the camp was over he had accepted Christ. They later married and have gone on for the Lord. It was a good beginning at our new and permanent location. Before this we had rented the Salvation Army camp near Wichita. We incorporated as Kansas Bible Camp to own this property. Karl Pfaff, Richard Burson, Ken Engle and I worked together that summer. I taught a daily lesson as well as being a counselor in a dorm. Marie had a class for the young children. Ken told of his missionary work in the Philippines and we had a missionary banquet one night. Russ Farwell was a big help in transporting children from Kansas City and in counseling.

Following the camps we had a Labor Day conference at the camp on Monday, Sept. 3 with people coming from Abilene, Elm Springs, Wichita and Hutchinson. Karl Pfaff and I spoke morning and afternoon and then we left for home. In the following years we have spent much time at the camp and I am still on the board (2003). Richard was a great director until his early death at 58. He loved children and had a tremendous sense of humor. Other younger men since then have directed the camp: John Bloom, Rick Mills and John Denny.

When I arrived home we began to advertise our house, still with a burden to move to El Paso or Albuquerque and to get more involved in the work in Mexico. If the Lord wanted us to move He would bring a buyer along. We had seen this happen before. We stayed active in the work, seeking to strengthen the assembly and having meetings. We had seen some saved; now it was a struggle to see them grow and become stable in their faith. It was a mixture of evangelism, shepherding and teaching.

That fall I read the life of Robert Chapman and was blessed. I wrote, "God knows I want to be a brother to everyone who is a child of God. I need to be more loving and tender with God's people, less critical. Today Marie and I read and prayed in the afternoon. We have many lessons to learn." The Lord has been very patient with us. On Oct. 29, 1956, I wrote, "Bought bread, butter and gas. Down to 11 cents again. Sometimes the financial leanness is a strain, subconsciously perhaps. I need more real faith. Thoughts of how it will be harder for me to get work the older I get, etc., come in to bother. My faith is often very weak." But then, over and over again, God would provide and faith would grow. God is faithful!

I was going up regularly to Ponca City for a Bible study on Tuesday nights. I did visitation in the neighborhood, giving out tracts and telling of the Bible study. But there was not much response for some time. At times there would be only Mrs. Secrest and one other Christian lady. But we prayed and persevered. Bill Secrest was still unsaved, but listening.

People looked at our house but no one bought. We were wondering and praying about what we should do. I was writing articles from time to time and these were being published in the UK in *Believer's Magazine* and *The Witness*, and also in the *Evangelical Quarterly*, a scholarly journal. *Light and Liberty and Interest* were publishing my articles in the States. *New Testament Church Organization* had been published here and also in India. I was very grateful to be able to have a writing ministry that could reach further afield.

In December I wrote: "Read a brief life history of John Olley—Chad, Africa—37 years without leaving Africa. My own heart was rebuked by selfishness. Once again consecrated myself to the Lord, prayed for greater usefulness, zeal. Felt my heart drawn again to Mexico, to help there as He leads. May the Lord lead us."

I had had rectal surgery in Wheaton which had not healed well, lots of scar tissue. So I had to have surgery again on Feb. 8, 1957. I had a good doctor who was of the old school. He said, "I do not charge doctors, nurses or ministers." We were most grateful that we only had the hospital bill to pay. Healing was painful but soon I was home on the 14th and recovering. Marie wrote: "The hospital bill was $138.30 and we had more than enough to pay it. How good & true is Philippians 4:19[1]. Am very full of thankfulness to Him tonight."

The Bible class in Ponca began to show more interest in March 1957. Through visits in the neighborhood I contacted the Jeff Morgans. He had been going from church to church seeking rest for his soul. His wife said to him, "Why don't you visit the Bible study down the street?" They were members of the Presbyterian Church but not saved. She came with him the first time but then she pulled back, but Jeff kept coming. After a time Jeff accepted Christ.

Later Doris Wear came, a vivacious, young woman, who was a receptionist at Continental Oil. She was a church member but unsaved. She listened well and in July turned to Christ. Doris was a good witness. When young men wished to date her she would say, "I will go out with you, if you will go with me to the Bible study!" She brought a number to the class and some were saved. Cecil Wood, a young attorney from Blackwell, came with her one night. We had a good talk and I gave him some tracts. The next week when he came to the study he said he was now saved! Cecil's folks began coming. One night after the class his mother rushed up to me and exclaimed, "Don, now I know I am saved. I see it now. I do believe." She too had accepted Christ.

I gave teaching on baptism but Jeff Morgan resisted taking that step. He insisted his previous baptism was enough. But one night after the study he abruptly said, "I want to be baptized!" When asked when he wanted to be baptized he said,

---

[1] *"But my God shall supply all your need according to his riches in glory by Christ Jesus."*

"Tonight!" We drove out to Lake Ponca and pointed the cars toward the lake to light up the shore and Jeff was baptized. We all rejoiced at his obedience. Later at another baptism the caretaker expressed some concern. He said that this was the city's drinking water and he was afraid the water would be contaminated by the sins washed away. We assured him that no sins would be left in the water! Christ's blood had cleansed them away. At times we had as many as twenty-seven at our Bible study and a number were saved. We had hoped to see an assembly begun there but Bill Secrest was unexpectedly transferred to Texas and others moved. We lacked a strong core to continue the work.

In June after a visit from missionary friends our children all came down with amoebic dysentery. So we were all put on medication to clear it up. The children did get rid of it more quickly than I did. That can be a persistent parasite. And in June we discovered that Marie was pregnant with our fifth child, an unexpected blessing!

In July we revisited the Chicago area and saw friends in Wheaton and Chicago with a number of opportunities to speak. The children enjoyed visits to the zoo and Natural History Museum, a good family time. Then it was on to Minnesota and visiting family. At a Norbie reunion I asked my grandmother if I could speak to the group of forty-two relatives; I had such a burden for my lost family. Grandma was a believer, although not well taught, and was happy for me to do this. I spoke on the lost son (Luke 15) and gave the gospel, along with my testimony. I felt a burden lifted. At least now they had heard the gospel. All were church members but most were very lost, trusting their infant baptism.

At various times I was asked to officiate at weddings, which are usually joyful occasions. In August I was asked to take Eloise Engle's wedding to Kevin Dyer. They were married in the country chapel near Abilene, where Eloise had grown up. Eloise had grown up going to Kansas Bible Camp and loved the Lord, a dear girl. Kevin made a good choice.

11

A New House & Bible Camp

The fall of 1957 we kept trying to sell our house, with no success. Marie wrote, "Soon it will be too late to make a move because of the baby due in January. Lord, lead us through circumstances." We finally decided that we should look at some larger houses locally. If the Lord wanted us to stay in Oklahoma City we did need a larger house with the baby coming. Our present house was very small.

We looked at a large, two story, older house at 1205 N. W. 34th Street. It was run down and was the closing of an estate. The owner had died of cancer and the house had been neglected for years. The realtor said, "The person who buys this will need to have vision!" But it had room, lots of room, four big bedrooms upstairs with a sleeping porch. Downstairs it had a nice kitchen, another big bathroom, a large dining room and living room that was 15' x 30'. It would be great for all of the entertaining that we did. As we looked at the house, Donna exclaimed with awe, "Our whole family can get in this bathroom!"

We decided we had the vision to renovate the house! On November 23 we signed a contract on the house for $8,300.00 and prayed for the sale of our house. We had only been home for a short time when a realtor came by with a contract for the sale of our house for $7,500.00. We had tried for nearly two years to sell our small house with the thought of moving down near Mexico and had no offers. The Lord confirmed our decision; He wanted us to stay in Oklahoma. About this time while reading through Ezekiel, God spoke to me through His words to Ezekiel, "For you are not sent to a people of unfamiliar speech and of hard language but to the house of Israel" (Ez. 3:5). The words gripped me as I accepted the fact that my ministry would be primarily in English.

We moved on December 16 and spent some days settling in. We hurried because the doctor said the baby could come early in January. Over the weeks and months I worked on the house. The floor had to be leveled, old wall paper removed and the walls painted. Later I would paint the siding of the house and put on new roofing. But gradually it took shape and became our most roomy, liveable house. We could go out through our hedge right into a city park. It was a great place to play, with a creek running through it with real, live crayfish in it. What a place to play cowboys and Indians! It also had a small swimming pool where our children learned to swim. They adjusted well to their new school and liked it.

We were interested in starting a camp in Oklahoma; the distance to Kansas Bible Camp made it difficult for some to come. I investigated the Lew Wentz Camp that was owned by Ponca City which they rented out to various groups. They had one week open in June and we decided to take it and to trust the Lord to supply the campers and staff that would be needed.

Our doctor was concerned about the baby's delayed arrival and finally had Marie take some castor oil and that started labor. Finally a baby boy weighing 8 lbs. 14 oz. was born on January 24. He was our third son and we named him Douglas. We now had five children and were very thankful that all were normal and healthy. We had prayed for each one from the time of conception and had given them to God. Our longing was that each would become a man or woman of God.

That summer (1958) we had our first camp in Oklahoma and named it Sooner Bible Camp. Oklahoma is often called the Sooner State because when the area was opened for homesteading some jumped the gun and came in early to stake out their claims. Because of Marie's camp experience she was willing to be the camp cook, being helped by several other ladies. We left baby Doug at home with Barbara Moffitt. Camp started June 1. Marie wrote, "Found the camp to be a beautiful place, main building and pool are on a high hill overlooking Lake Ponca. Lovely cool breeze. Got settled in a cabin (they are octagonal and built all of stone) and got supper underway."

For 25 years Marie would be the head cook and did a beautiful job. The women loved working with her even though the work could be hard and hot. Now the kitchen is air conditioned but it was not then. We had 53 to feed that year with 37 campers; it was an encouraging beginning. And some of the campers professed Christ. We had two lessons, one for the younger campers and another for the older. In more recent years we have been able to have two weeks of camp with separate the age groups. Hundreds have gone through the camp. Now we are having grandparents who went through camp bringing their grandchildren! I taught daily lessons and directed the camp for 25 years. Then I felt I should turn the directorship over to other younger men and they have done a good job. Rob Lindsted, Toby O'Bannon, Baer Bell and Dan Moffitt have helped with the directing. I have continued helping with the teaching. Herschel Martindale helped with the teaching that first year and others have helped faithfully through the years.

In October 1958 I finished reading the book on Jim Elliot's life. He and I had been together for a year at Wheaton. I was in graduate school and he was a senior. We had kept in touch since then. "I finished Jim Elliott's life today and was blessed, stirred and torn with sorrow. He and I so different, yet hearts beating in unison so often. What an ache, a fierce, crushing ache of heart to know he is gone! My thinking is often confused about how much does God order, permit, restrain? ... God, give me faith to appropriate Romans 8:28, to believe and not to doubt. Our God, Who knows us, awesome, searching thought, and loves us with all the melting warmth of His Great Heart, He will work out for good the woof and warp of life's variegated fabric."

"I am 35 today. The family were all sweet and loving at breakfast. Sang for me and the boys brought in 2 gifts: a pair of shorts made by Marie and a belt. Girls will give me theirs later.

"They are dear, sweet children. The Lord has blessed me

richly. I deserve none of it."

"Oh my God, I write from a full heart with the tears coursing down my face. These things I ask: 1. A life more like the Lord Jesus; unselfish, loving, kind, gracious, holy. Lord keep my thinking pure. What fearful lusts and passions rage within this heart at times. A calm surface but underneath a turmoil of vicious currents of thought ... Help me to live a more happy, serene life. Keep me from dark, introspective probings of the soul. 2. Then for the work: A life more filled with Thy Spirit, more radiant, throbbing with all the vigor and beauty of Divine life."

On July 14, 1959, we found a note on our bed written by Dorothy. "Dear Mother and Daddy, I am sorry I was so bad in curch. I will try very hurd to be good next time. I asked the Jesus to forgive me. Love, Dorothy" The spelling could be improved but we appreciated the spirit of the note!

In May of 1959 Donna came downstairs one evening and dressed in her nightie and rather bashfully said, "I want to be baptized, Daddy." She seems very sweet, earnest and understanding. I talked a little of the meaning of baptism, confession of Christ, a renunciation of the world, etc. Lord, we give our children to Thee. May they be devoted, useful vessels in Thy tender hand, here or abroad. They are Thine. Later in June she was baptized by Frank Moffitt, along with other young people, a happy day in our life. "I wept to see Donna baptized, our first. May her life honor the Lord Jesus and bring much joy to Him."

That July we had tent meetings again with Herschel. A violent thunderstorm ripped the tent stakes loose and tore the top. Everything was soaking wet. We managed to get it up and dried out enough to continue the meetings. Oklahoma weather can be violent. A tent man said that $75.00 would repair the tent. I always felt sad when we took the tent down, thinking that perhaps if we tried a little longer we would see more fruit. A lady named Mary Ann told us later that she had been saved during those meetings. We also had a broadcast at that time called "Truth for Today." That summer was also busy with camps in Oklahoma and Kansas. I usually counseled a cabin as well as teaching—a very tiring week!

In September I was backing the car into our driveway and

A NEW HOUSE & BIBLE CAMP

felt a thump. Thinking I had run over a log I pulled forward and then I heard screams. Doug had stepped out from behind a porch pillar and I had run over him!

"Dougie was lying face down and crushed into the cement. My heart failed but he was breathing and screaming. We hurriedly took him to Dr. Kimball and he examined him and took x-rays. There were no broken bones! The doctor said, "He is very, very fortunate." I had missed his head but came close. The doctor said to watch him to see if he passed any blood. He proved to be unharmed. I wrote, "The tire's tread is livid on his flesh." Surely the Lord was good and his sister realized she needed to watch him more closely.

We had been given a kitten that we named "Chica." "Often when I read the Word she will jump up on my lap. The other day while I knelt in prayer she climbed upon my back, licked and arranged my hair, then settled down for a rest on my shoulders, purring her contented song. Life has many simple pleasures. I marvel at the perfect way God has made her."

1959 came to a close with a profound sense of the Lord's goodness and care. We looked at Doug, happy and well, and were most thankful. The other children were growing and healthy. As a family we were very blessed; all of our financial needs had been met. We were aware of God's grace. "How wretched this old heart is, selfish, arrogant, envious, quick-tempered. Something of the wonder of God's grace in saving me swept over me again. Oh, the wonder of His love!"

1960 was a busy year again. We started the year with a watch night service in Guthrie, a happy way to begin a new year. We also had our annual Sunday School program with about 60 present. I had been having meetings in Cushing in a home for some time, but there was not enough interest to see a permanent work done. In March I had hernia surgery and made a good recovery. Then in April the Moffitts learned that Frank was being transferred to Illinois in the near future. This was a tremendous loss to our assembly. Frank and his family had become pillars in the work. May the Lord build His work here was our prayer.

In May I was at the Wichita conference speaking with David

Kirk and Richard Burson. It was a good conference, a time of happy fellowship. Our camp at Ponca City in June was a success with 64 campers, altogether with staff about 90. Some professed Christ. And then there was camp later in Kansas.

Ben Tuininga, a fellow teacher at Emmaus, had started directing a small camp in Northern Minnesota called Story Book Lodge on Cedar Island Lake. Ben decided to expand the work and to start a teen camp. He asked me to come and be the Bible teacher.

So we began working with that Teen Camp on August 1, 1960. It was a two week camp and small that first year, about 25-30 campers but a great week. The next year George Lartz, a high school teacher from Sheboygan came to help. For thirty years we worked together with the teens and saw much blessing in souls being saved and young Christians encouraged. Ben's wife Jean was a tremendous asset with her nature hikes and animated story telling. She has gone home to be with the Lord and Ben is now retired but the work goes on well. From the first the camp has run on a faith basis with no fees charged. The Lord has provided; new buildings have been erected and the camp is full all summer. In recent years I have gone to speak at Family Camps.

That first year I wrote: "It is beautiful, northern Minnesota, tall, fragrant pines, stately white birch almost startling in their contrast, and delightfully blue lakes everywhere. Nights are cool and days are pleasantly warm." I was born in Minnesota and was delighted to contribute a little to the Lord's work in my home state. We were able to visit family on the way to camp and could thus strengthen ties to my father and brother, although neither were saved then.

That year too I was introduced to the camp sauna. After the campers were in bed, Ben, Roland Thompson and I took a sauna and got steaming hot. I wrote, "Then after soaping down you rush out—bare naked and jump into the lake. I thought it would be an awful shock as we three rushed headlong for the lake. But the water felt warm and deliciously refreshing. I wish I could preserve the beauty of the night. The water was breathlessly still. The moon climbed lazily into the sky and cast a silver spell over all. It was with genuine reluctance that we got out and dressed. As we climbed the slope a frog croaked a throaty benediction." Our family has many fond memories of Story Book!

Then later that August I was speaking at a Jr. High camp and also a Sr. High camp at Kansas Bible Camp. The Lord blessed with some professing Christ.

That fall Ben wanted to go to the Workers' Conference, a conference for workers and elders that was to be held in San Diego. He wanted me to go with him, so we drove out. It was a pleasant trip, driving to El Paso on Oct 31 (690 miles) and then on to Tucson the next day. The following day we drove on to San Diego. We had good fellowship on the trip. Ben and I were in agreement on many issues.

The conference was good. John Walden and others of us spoke. I little knew that this would mark the beginning of a lengthy involvement with the conference. I began to go every year. Later I was asked to serve on the conference committee. When William Murray the executive secretary died, they asked me to serve in that capacity. While opposed to any centralized authority, I did see the value of workers and elders coming together for teaching, fellowship and encouragement. Many labor in smaller assemblies and these conferences broaden their vision and encourage them to press on in their service for the Lord.

The next few years passed quickly. We were able to build on a nice, modest chapel in the front of our building. We applied for a loan to a local bank. When I talked to the loan officer, he said, "We cannot loan to a small, independent church. The whole situation is too insecure." But we prayed and he called us back. He said, "This is against our policy but the bank has decided to loan you the money!" We found a Christian builder who did a good job and we rejoiced when it was all finished.

Marie's father died in his sleep in January 1963. We went out for the funeral and it was a bitterly cold trip in our VW bug. Those cars were notorious for having poor heaters. It was a sad time; yet there was joy in knowing that he was with the Lord. In the following months Marie's mother began to urge us to consider moving to California. Marie was her only daughter and she longed for her to live closer. She said, "There is lots of spiritual need in California." One could not argue with that.

The Moffitts were living in Salem, Illinois, and encouraged Ben Tuininga and me to come for an evangelistic series. In April we had two weeks of meetings with a number of strangers out. One lady professed Christ through home visits. The Moffitts would like to have seen an assembly begun there but later they were transferred back to Oklahoma. On the way home we visited the Bill Howells in Brookfield, Missouri, and encouraged them in their concern to see an assembly begun there. Since then a healthy work has been established. Then it was on to the Lawrence Littlefields in Kansas City and some meetings at the Spruce Hill Chapel before going home.

We had good camps that summer; at Sooner we had 92 campers. Later in June I was with the Banks in Littleton, Colorado, for Daily Vacation Bible School. The assembly rented a gym in a grade school for the week. There was a good turnout and the saints were encouraged. The closing program was on Friday night with 130 present, a good opportunity to preach the gospel. Then there was the teen camp in Minnesota in July and camps in Kansas during August. I spoke on the life of Christ. "The Lord gave me real joy in teaching of the Saviour. How good it is to rejoice in the perfection of His person, the beauty of His teaching, the gloriousness of His death and resurrection. The young folk seemed helped. I trust they will love Him more for having come. Marie helped with cooking and crafts."

In October I had meetings in Springfield, Missouri, and stayed with the Ron Millers. During the meetings, "a little, old, bent-over widow lady came up to me, shook my hand firmly, slipping a $5.00 bill into it and said, 'You'll never know how much these meetings have meant to me.' There were tears in her eyes as she turned away. Times like these make it all seem worth while."

Later in October I took a trip back to Washington, D.C., for the Workers' Conference. On the way I visited dear friends in Memphis and Murfreesboro where I stayed at the Jack Weatherfords. Then it was on to Asheville, North Carolina, and a stay with the James Innes family, a godly elder in the assembly. There was a brief visit in Raleigh with the Chappells, with meetings in these various towns.

A NEW HOUSE & BIBLE CAMP

Then I drove to Newport News where I stayed with the Willie Millars. "Sat. (19th) I drove to Newport News and the memories rolled over me like the waves of the sea as I crossed the James R. bridge into the town. Belle gave me a hug and Willie a warm hand. It is over 20 years since I used to stay with them. . . .Their home was a place of warmth and love when I was a lonely sailor boy." We drove out to the harbor. "Anchored in Hampton Roads were about four carriers, one the *Enterprise*, largest ever built—a cruiser, destroyers and smaller craft. It was thrilling to see. Memories, memories."

Four of us shipped out from the assembly there at the same time, Jack, Arthur, Willie and I. Willie never came back, killed in action on a carrier in the Pacific. "His mother came up to me and gripped my hand. Her body shook with emotion. She tried to speak but could say little. Poor soul! My heart ached for her." It had been twenty years but the wounds were still tender. "I have been spared. God's will, God's purpose, the mystery of life. Oh, Father God, use me increasingly for Thyself. I have been spared to live."

From there I drove to Washington for the Workers' Conference. At this time I was asked to serve on the Conference Committee which plans the conferences. T. B. Gilbert, William Murray, Edwin Fesch, Ben Tuininga and I made up the group. Will acted as the executive secretary and when he died they asked me to assume his duties. It has been a joy to work with these dear men and others through the years, God's choice saints. It was a great conference.

On my way home to Oklahoma I visited Chicago and Emmaus. It was a good time of fellowship with Bill MacDonald, Paul Flint, Bill Anderson and John Harper, the current staff. I then stopped in Salem to see the Moffitts and to be with them for their Sunday meeting in their home. But I had a terrific bout of amoebic dysentery and left early to drive home. It was a miserable 600 mile trip; I pulled in at midnight, exhausted. Then it was off to the doctor for another course of treatment.

Marie's mother wanted us to come out for Christmas 1963. It would be the first time the whole family had been together since 1946 and now her husband was gone. We made the trip out and it was a happy time with family and friends in the area. We revisited Santa Barbara and friends there in the little assembly. How we longed to see a stronger work there where students from Westmont and the University could see a vibrant, New Testament assembly functioning. "My heart was moved to consider Santa Barbara as a place to move." Marie's mother was urging us to consider moving back to California. Perhaps it was time for the assembly in Oklahoma City to be on its own.

After returning to Oklahoma we put our house on the market. Our children did not want to move. "We had prayed for leading and guidance that night. I guess none of us really want to move. We have a comfortable, roomy house, nice Christian friends, sweet fellowship in the assembly. It would be much easier just to stay. However, we believe the Lord would have us move and help in another area." We would leave the sale of the house in his hands. The question was where? Should we stay in Oklahoma and the Midwest or move further west?

Sooner Bible Camp

Tom McCullagh family

Kansas Bible Camp 1958

Tuinigas family 1956

Donald Norbie family 1962

Richard Burson family 1950

12

A Difficult Decision

In March of 1964 I was at the young people's conference in Hutchinson with Gordon Wakefield and Karl Pfaff. It was an encouraging time. Arriving home I wrote: "Two checks came over the weekend totaling $105.00. We are most thankful to the Lord. Now we can pay the house payment and a gas bill on hand. The flesh rebels against the discipline of faith; yet how we need the humbling experience of utter dependence upon the Living God."

Later in March I drove down to McAllen, Texas, to visit the Secrests. Bill had been transferred down there and they wanted to have some Bible studies in their home, remembering the blessing we had seen in Ponca City. I spent about two weeks there, visiting and having Bible studies. During a visit a man asked me how I served the Lord. I told him of the simple pathway of faith, trusting the Lord for our needs, and also described how a New Testament assembly functions. He said, "I know of another man who served the Lord that way." I said, "You do!" He said, "Yes, the apostle Paul!" But he was anchored in his church. I prayed, "Oh that there might come into existence here in the Valley a simple, fervent New Testament assembly." I drove home by way of Houston and saw old friends there.

In April I had a week of meetings in Springfield, Missouri. After a meeting I wrote: "The Lord gave real help; the words came freely, no hard pumping. In a sense there is intense labor—at the close I was soaked with perspiration. Yet in a way too it is effortless—one is so possessed and carried along by the Holy Spirit. Thank you, Lord." I spent the days in visitation and spoke every night. "After the last meeting Albert (Bud) Steele said to me, 'Well, you trampled all over again tonight and tore me up! But I need it.' He thanked me and gave me a check."

In May we had a series of gospel meetings at our chapel with Tom McCullagh; hard driving, earnest preaching. A woman professed Christ and seemed very real. At the end an older couple also said they had been saved after a home visit we had made.

Our house was still on the market and unsold. We longed to see the assembly on the south side more supportive of our newer assembly. But one man in leadership there opposed the work and discouraged any interest others might have had. Then on May 18 we did sign a contract on our house, subject to approval by the F. H. A. Now we would have to make a decision about moving. "How cast upon the Lord we are! May He guide us as He has promised. Oklahoma, Texas, Arizona or California! How great the need is everywhere."

Sunday, June 7, I wrote: "Today is our wedding anniversary of 17 years. I have been very thankful for my wife, her industry and sweet steadiness. I have been going over her many good points and virtues in my mind and have been very thankful." The week before, we had our Sooner camp, our largest yet. We had 118 campers and with staff we fed 138. It was a great week with some discipline problems but with 15 or 20 professions of faith. If we moved I still planned to stay involved and to direct the camp.

Finally on June 9 the house sale went through; the loan was approved. Rather reluctantly we signed the papers; we would need to move out by July 1. "Marie and I spent some good time in prayer this morning, searching our hearts, crying to God for leading. We do not want to move to a new location for selfish reasons." The news stirred our assembly and special prayer was held. "Jim Nelson broke down as he prayed, thanking God for us and feeling a need of special grace to carry on the work. It is blessed to know we are loved and will be missed. May the Lord

A DIFFICULT DECISION

strengthen and build the work." The deal was finally closed on the 18th. Now our time was short. What should we do with our furniture and belongings? We were not even sure of where we would move. We located a furniture van for sale with a 16 foot box. A Christian family had bought it to move down from Iowa; we bought it for $900.00 and loaded most of our belongings into it on June 20. Dear Dewey Smith, a spiritual son of ours, helped me load the truck.

Tuesday, June 23, there was a fellowship dinner in our honor. Some came from the other assembly and there was a meeting in the chapel after the dinner. "Ralph Burrs stood up and said he was sure he could speak for the saints there in expressing appreciation for us and our labors. He spoke very warmly." Ralph was from the south side meeting. I spoke also using Paul's words to the Ephesian elders in Acts 20. Then Jim Nelson spoke, expressing their dependence upon the Lord. "Many tears were shed. Chiquita and Maxine especially wept and wept. Dear souls. How close we are to one another in the bonds of Christ." They were two women we had seen come to the Lord who were very dear to us. It was very hard for us to think of leaving.

The truck was finally packed and parked at the Smiths while we went off to camp. June 25 we drove to Hutchinson and stayed over night at the camp. The next day we drove to Minneapolis, 670 miles, a long, hard day with five children in the station wagon. We spent Sunday with friends in Minneapolis, the Jacobsons, and I spoke at Sunnyside and the N. E. assembly. The next day we drove to Story Book for another camp session. "The timber and lakes make a delightful combination. We have about 85 campers, a full camp." I had the joy of leading two brothers to the Lord on the same day. Lee, the older one, had just graduated from high school and was troubled about his sin. "He is a Lutheran. When he went to the pastor with a burdened heart he was told to forget it; he was one of their best boys. Yet Lee said, 'He didn't know how rotten I was inside.'" It was a joy to see him turn to the Lord and to come to know peace and forgiveness. Later that day his brother Tom also trusted Christ. Others were saved as well.

After camp we took a trip east. We wanted to see a number

of old friends. In Grand Haven, Michigan, we stayed with the Ken Ruiters, an old Navy friend. Then it was on to Obie Snider's farm in Pennsylvania. Mary Ann was T. B. Gilbert's daughter and a friend from Tucson days. We visited Gettysburg on our way to D.C., giving the children some history lessons along the way. In D.C. we stayed with Fred and Sara Miller, who had been in our assembly in Oklahoma. We had a lovely time with them and were able to see some of the sights of that great city. I am not sure that our children appreciated all of the grandeur of our capitol but we did. It was very hot and humid. That Sunday I spoke at the New Hampshire Chapel, where the Millers were in fellowship.

Leaving there we retraced our steps to Minnesota and visited my father, who was still unsaved. We did have some opportunities to witness to him and his family. From there we went to the assembly camp at Lake Koronis, Minnesota. Len Lindsted spoke to the grade school camp and I had 75 teenagers. With the adults we numbered about 375. Some of the teenagers did turn to the Lord in salvation. It was a good week. Minnesota has always been near to my heart. We visited other family members in the Willmar area before heading for home.

When we arrived in Oklahoma, Herschel Martindale called me from Texas and pleaded with me to visit Odessa. The assembly there was being divided by Witness Lee and his Little Flock teaching. Because we were due to head west shortly, the only way I could visit Odessa was to fly. I felt a little anxious about flying; my last flight was in the Navy 20 years before! But the flight went well. Henry Lieb and Damon Holmes picked me up and we visited at length. The assembly was very upset and confused. Francis Ball had been a leading elder in the work and he had followed Witness Lee in his teaching. Lee had gained an entrance into the assembly by saying he was a disciple of Watchman Nee and had some meetings with the believers. We visited Francis for four hours, trying to dissuade him, but he was convinced of Lee's teaching on the local church, a partial rapture, 1, 000 years of darkness, etc. Naomie, his wife, was all upset with him over this teaching. The marriage broke up later and Francis moved to California to work with Lee, becoming a loyal follower.

A DIFFICULT DECISION

Francis had done most of the speaking and the men were confused and finally decided to sell the building and to disband. I urged them to continue meeting as a group but they were too discouraged and most decided to go to the various existing churches. They had been too dependent on the Balls. A few decided to continue meeting in the Lieb's home. We had the Lord's supper and a time of teaching before I had to fly out. In time though the little group would disband, lacking good, strong leadership. It is not easy to start an assembly.

When I arrived home we left for California. We would need to get settled before school started and felt we should investigate California. Marie's mother was still urging us to move closer to her. Since my mother was gone we felt some obligation to care for her. We drove straight through—a long, hot trip and stayed with Grandma while we scouted out the area. "In this matter of moving and finding the Lord's mind it is so easy to be moved by one's selfish desires and interests. May the Lord spare us from this." We were urged to consider the area up around Thousand Oaks or Camarillo, fifty miles north of Los Angeles. Some families were driving in from that area to the West Valley assembly in the San Fernando valley. Van Hairgrove, a retired Marine, lived in Camarillo. He said, "Don, for years I have been praying that an assembly might get started in this area."

Christians in Phoenix had also urged us to consider moving there. We had previously considered Norman, Oklahoma, the university town, and Albuquerque. It was a time of much prayer and indecision. I did not like California culture, much preferring the more conservative Midwest. California boasted that it was on the cutting edge of societal change and we did not like the change that was taking place and was about to accelerate. I have since decided that if one does not have peace about a move it is better to stay where you are!

We left California driving east to Phoenix and stopped for lunch at a rest stop in Indio. It was fearfully hot but we had a time of prayer and finally "decided to turn around, go back to Camarillo to spend one year or more to see if an assembly can be formed." Marie would be able to spend more time with her mother but I was concerned for our children. That night,

Saturday, August 29, we rented a motel in Camarillo. The next day I went to the West Valley assembly with the Hairgroves and told the saints we were moving to Camarillo. They were delighted to welcome us and wanted to see a work begun out that way.

We had looked at a house earlier and now put an offer on it that was accepted. We moved in on Tuesday and the Christians loaned us some furniture temporarily. Then on Thursday, Sept. 3, I left on the bus for Albuquerque and their conference. Tom McCullagh, T. B. Gilbert and Brother Dresch from San Antonio were also speakers. I stayed with Eddie and Pauline Jeanjaquet, dear friends from years past. It was a good conference; I spoke on 2 Timothy. Tuesday, Sept. 8, I caught the bus for Oklahoma City and arrived there that night.

I got the truck ready for the trip and was with the saints for their prayer meeting and one last farewell. "My heart was heavy as I thought of leaving them. I spoke on John 13." I left early on Thursday morning, Sept. 10, and began driving. "I must confess that the long trip with a heavily loaded truck with nearly smooth tires makes me a little anxious. May the Lord take me safely."

Because the engine had new rings I took it easy to Vega, New Mexico, where I had the oil changed. Then I could drive a little harder. I made it to Grants the first day and got a motel at 11:00 p.m., 641 miles covered. The next day I had an early start and was now used to the truck. I had a meal in Needles at 6:00 a.m. where it was still 104 degrees. I decided to drive on through the desert at night while it was cooler. I went through L.A. at 1:00 a.m., "the freeways humming with traffic. Does the city ever sleep?" "Finally the truck grumbled down the Camarillo grade and I was home about 2:15 a.m. I covered 837 miles that day, really too far." But praise the Lord, I made it safely with no truck trouble.

The truck was unloaded and we settled in. Our new house was smaller than our Oklahoma house but we would adjust. Sunday night we began a Bible study in the Hairgroves' home. David Gomes, a Navy man, and his wife, Jalna came. "May the Lord give us the joy of seeing a work established here." We en-

A DIFFICULT DECISION

rolled the children in school. They missed Oklahoma, especially Donna and Dale. In fact, we all did but we needed to adjust to our new setting. I realized later how hard it is for children to adjust to a move, leaving all of their old friends behind.

In October I had to go east for the Workers' Conference. I stopped in Tucson, El Paso and Odessa. It was hot across the California desert, about 110 degrees. "I enjoyed the solitary driving time to think, meditate, pray and sing. The Lord was near and sweet." In Tucson I visited our old house, now the office for a trailer park, and the memories came tumbling through my mind. How much had happened since those days! "Life is slipping by with its heartaches and joys. There is change on every hand. Only the mountains stand, solid and unchanging, reassuring in their stability. The mountains that guard Tucson look the same. How good to know our Lord's presence with His people is compared to such (Ps. 125:1-2)."

I spent several days in Odessa, longing to see the group encouraged and determined to go on. I stayed with the Henry Liebs, a dear family with whom I became very close. Sunday we had a full schedule of meetings and a happy time. However, I was troubled with another attack of amoebic dysentery, leaving me very weak. "The doctor will have to start me on another course of treatment when I get to Oklahoma City. October 13"? Today is my birthday 41 years old. How quickly life slips through one's fingers! How many more years will the Lord give me to live and to serve Him?" The Christians in Odessa with tears thanked me for coming.

Then it was on to Dallas and Oklahoma City where I got my prescription refilled. From there I went east to Murfreesboro to stay at Jack Weatherford's charming old home, arriving on the 16th. The Gilberts were living in Murfreesboro and had us over, delightful fellowship. I wrote during that stay: "The Lord has been showing me the depths of fearful wickedness in my heart, the insatiable lust, the deceptiveness, the rationalizing that goes on to defend self. How utterly corrupt the natural heart is! How sweet, how wonderfully sweet, to know the cleansing forgiveness of the Lord, flowing over the soul like pure, clean water. How gracious of the Lord to pick us up and to use us."

There were also meetings at Shelbyville and time with David Main. Then Monday T.B. Gilbert and I left Murfreesboro for the Workers' conference at Winston-Salem, North Carolina. It was a great conference with some dear men of God present: Peter Pell, August Van Ryn, Lester Wilson, Welcome Detweiler, Harold MacKay and others.

From there I went down to Hinton, West Virginia, where I stayed with the Harry Pilkingtons, students from our Toronto days. They had a young people's conference at a nearby lake and I was to speak. About 75 young people came and I took up the book of Philippians; it was a good time. That night I wrote: "I surely miss Marie and the children. At times I have a fierce hunger for her body, to kiss her, to embrace her, to love her. However, often too, as now, there is a deep loneliness for her companionship, to hear her voice, to share thoughts and experiences. How I could wish I were home. Yet this is the Lord's work and I would not feel sorry for myself. *'Even Christ pleased not Himself.'"*

After the conference I made my way back to Murfreesboro, then to Memphis and to Oklahoma City for several days. I stayed with the Smiths and it was a joy to be with the believers again. Then I drove on to Albuquerque, Mesa and finally home, with meetings at the various stops. It was so good to be home with the family again. On Nov. 24 we had a meeting of a few families in the area to discuss and to pray about the starting of a new assembly. We are praying for love and unity as we begin the work. We were having weekly Bible studies in our area and going to West Valley for the Sunday morning meetings.

New Year's eve a number of families were invited to the Dave Hunts for a meal and fellowship. It was a delightful way to end the old year. There was the feeling that Thousand Oaks was a central place for the new assembly to gather. A building became available to rent and we met on January 22 in the home of Dwayne Emery to arrange for the beginning of the assembly. David Gomes, Jim Elrod, Van Hairgrove, D. Emery, Cal Buchser and Herb Meyer were present. West Valley was happy to see a work begin out our way. We would call ourselves the Thousand Oaks Bible Fellowship. Sunday, February 7 was our first meet-

A DIFFICULT DECISION

ing, a time of joy and anticipation of future blessing in the work. We had the Lord's Supper at 9:30 a.m. and at 11:00 a.m. a Family Bible Hour with classes for the children. The Lord blessed and in time other families were added.

In March I had to make a trip east, stopping at Tucson, El Paso and Odessa. I especially wanted to spend some time in Odessa to try to encourage the demoralized Christians there. I tried to encourage them to evangelize and to be optimistic for the future. From there I drove to Wichita Falls to visit the Dave Silvers, a couple I had married years before. He was in the air force, flying B-52's, and Dave gave me a tour of one of these aircraft. Then it was on to Oklahoma City. I wrote: "Oklahoma looked good. Vast productive fields, no bumper-to-bumper traffic on highways, fields green carpeted with a lush stand of wheat, white-faced cattle contentedly grazing. It was coming home again."

My days in Oklahoma were busy with visiting and meetings. There were shepherding visits to the various Christians and contacts we had. I had a good visit with Jack Spencer; his wife Maxine had been saved previously but Jack was stubborn. I pleaded again with him to accept Christ. There were tears in his eyes but he said, "I can't let go!" Jack loved his liquor and it would destroy him. He died, driving drunk, hit by a big truck. They called me and I flew back for his funeral, one of the saddest I have ever taken. I left for home on April 17. One day I drove 700 miles from Lubbock to Phoenix, too much driving! In Lubbock I stayed with Jim Schooler and we had a meeting with the assembly. "California is at the end of things. It means more traveling for me and I can't say I like this."

Because of my involvement in the Midwest with camps and ties to the assemblies, every summer would mean long trips back there. There were always the camps in Oklahoma, Kansas and Minnesota that were close to my heart. Then there was the Workers' Conference in the fall, which usually alternated between the east coast and the central states. And then there were conferences where I was asked to speak in various places. It involved much driving, but it was across the picturesque Southwest with its magnificent mountains and deserts.

We spent much time with the new assembly, visiting, doing tract work and door-to-door work. But it was not too productive in terms of souls being saved. People were generally affluent and materialistic, pleasure oriented. But the Lord did give us some souls. In time elders were recognized in the assembly and there was a good spirit of harmony.

In May, 1965 Marie and I visited Bill W. and his wife in the San Fernando Valley. Bill was an old friend from Westmont days. He and I were both Greek majors. He was the president of his class and very active in Christian work. I had gone to Wheaton for an M.A. and he followed and then went on to the University of Chicago to get his Ph.D. While there he became enamored with Greek philosophy. As we talked I discovered he had left his Christian faith and was now an advocate of natural theology.

It was an upsetting evening for me; I loved Bill but he was now an apostate. "May the Lord keep my thinking. There are many things I don't know or understand completely, yet I do know the Saviour and the reality of His resurrection. To Him I cling when unbelieving doubts would erode faith. Without revelation in the Word and in the Son, there is no certainty; there is no absolute truth."

That summer we again had good camps in Oklahoma and Minnesota. At Lake Koronis we shared a cabin with Colin Anderson and his family. It was our first contact with him since Toronto days where he was a student. It was gratifying to see him again, now as a gifted teacher. He spoke to the adults and I spoke to the Teens. It was a good camp with some being saved. Then in August I was at Kansas Bible Camp again with 114 campers and a week of blessing. I took up the Life of Christ. From there we went to Oklahoma City for time with the assembly, trying to encourage them before setting off for home. We were gone much of the summer. Now it was time to get busy in Thousand Oaks again. We drove straight through, over the desert at night, and had a safe trip home with no car trouble on the whole trip. I had one more camp that month, Verdugo Pines, in S. California. Again the Lord gave blessing with some accepting Christ.

A DIFFICULT DECISION

The Children's Home in Culver City was being closed because of state regulations. Some brethren in the area decided to use the property for a one year Bible school and classes started that fall. Earl Fries had been a student of mine in Toronto and since those days had been a public school teacher. He was asked to be the principal and he approached me about coming down to help with the teaching. I drove down Thursday morning and had classes then and Friday morning, coming home on Friday afternoon. They named it the Culver City Bible School. I taught Doctrine and Christian evidences, heartily enjoying the classes. Just recently a woman came up to me at Kansas Bible Camp and said she had been one of my students then and had profited greatly. I had not seen her in over thirty years; it was so good to see her going on for the Lord.

That October I again had to go east to Baltimore for the Workers' Conference. I made stops along the way in Tucson, Odessa, Dallas and Oklahoma City, having meetings with the saints. Then it was on to Wheaton and Cleveland, where we stayed at Robbie Pile's home. John Mills was having meetings there, a student from Toronto days who has become a good teacher. It was a joy to renew that friendship. Then it was on to Baltimore and the conference. "I was asked to serve as Conf. Comm. Secretary and felt I should accept. Wm. Murray is no longer able to carry on with this. It will mean extra work but it is a position where I trust I can be of help and an influence for good. May the Lord give me wisdom and strength."

After a good conference I started the long drive home, taking Ben Tuininga as far as Chicago. I also stopped in Springfield, Ill., Oklahoma City, Albuquerque and Kingman on my way to California. There had been a small assembly in Kingman since 1920, only about 12 met regularly. Their chapel was a converted house; I stayed in one of the rooms. There has to be energetic leadership with vision or a work will not grow and will ultimately die.

In November we took the students down to Ensenada, Mexico, for several days to help the missionaries we knew there: McNeeley, Thames and Gill. They had messages from the missionaries, did tract work and were exposed to the poverty and dirt in which much of the world lives. While there my amoebic dysentery acted up and this continued for several days until I got on medication again. It left me weak and exhausted. "I am to be on this medication for 45 days, hopefully this will clear it up."

In December we moved from our house on Sharon Drive to a larger house at 1592 Anacapa. We had to have a little more room for our family. We still missed that large house we had in Oklahoma.

In the spring I made a trip back to Oklahoma and had a series of meetings with our assembly there, trying to encourage them. "The leadership is weak. One man who has been saved the longest is up and down spiritually and this discourages the others. Secrests have moved back to Ponca City and now two other families are meeting with them as an assembly. It was good to visit them and also the assemblies in Guthrie and the south side of Okla. City. Then it was home by way of Waco, Odessa and El Paso. I drove straight home from El Paso, 875 miles!" It makes me tired thinking of it!

In June we had a good Vacation Bible School in Thousand Oaks with 107 out for our closing program, an encouraging time. 1966 was filled with the usual activities and camps Sooner, Story Book, Lake Koronia and Kansas Bible Camp. We did have an additional camp that summer in Colorado at Camp Elim, up above Colorado Springs. It was a college-age camp and we made it a study camp with two hours of class morning and afternoon, assigned home work and a paper to write. Roger Cocking and I were the teachers. Roger took up 1 and 2 Timothy and the Church. I took up basic doctrines and Daniel. Jim Wright directed the camp and did a great job. A college student named Don Neilson was there. He had been recently saved and was keen for the Lord. He became interested in our daughter, Donna, and they struck up a correspondence. Little did we know that this would ripen into love and marriage.

"Saturday night Don Neilson, Brooky Stockton and I prayed together until 11:00 p.m. a wonderful time of earnest prayer around the camp fire under the stars. Dear, earnest fellows, God bless them." During a lean time financially I wrote: "I believe, I must believe, that the living God of heaven can supply without appeals and without a compromise of principle. Then dark doubts. There is no God. It is all a myth. Your needs have been met by accident, by chance. Seventeen years of accidents, of chances, that have marvelously met our needs, year after year, with no hint from us of these needs? Forgive me, Lord. Strengthen my faith."

We were delighted to hear that the Moffitts were being transferred back to Oklahoma and would once again be able to help with the North Side Assembly. This was a real encouragement to them. Frank and Barbara are such dear, faithful people.

Finally we were home after a long, busy summer. We were gone for ten weeks as a family. I still marvel that we traveled with seven people in that station wagon with all of our luggage. But it was a good summer and profitable spiritually; a number professed Christ. It was back in the routine of home and getting the children back in school. Then in October I had to go east again for the Workers' Conference. It was in Flint, Michigan, that year and I had good visits with friends in Grand Haven and Grand Rapids. My car broke down in Wilcox, Arizona, and I had to lay over for extensive repairs: two new pistons, rings and inserts. That was an expensive delay, but the Lord had provided. On my birthday I wrote: "Lord, I know not how much longer you will give me to live. I would ask for long life, if it be your will, even until the coming of the Lord. I ask for spiritual discernment in your Word to discover spiritual truths and principles to govern my individual life and the corporate life of the assembly. I pray for courage to stand by principles and convictions if need be alone. (Thank you, Lord, I am not alone.) I ask, Father, for spiritual children, for the privilege of taking younger men under my wing to encourage them in the life of faith."

After the conference it was the long trip home and back into the activities of the assembly. We began the new year, 1967, with a special time of prayer for the work of the assembly. I also started my classes again at Culver City on Thursday and Friday, staying overnight at the school. I heard the magazine *Light and Liberty*, which had published many of my articles, was closing down. This saddened me. "There needs to be a magazine with a conservative stance, yet progressive in being willing to examine and consider new ideas and methods—willing to discuss controversial and contemporary issues."

On March 30 I had to have rectal surgery again. Dr. Morikone, our family doctor, did the surgery and did a good job, better than the previous specialists. And he graciously charged nothing. Thank you, Lord. I witnessed to him often and he may have been a Christian, at least very favorable. When we left the hospital we were able to pay the complete bill. Healing took place slowly and I was soon able to be active again.

After Sooner Bible Camp, the first week of June, we hurried home for Donna's graduation. She was a good student and was granted two scholarships to college. That fall she began college in Ventura and lived at home.

In the spring of 1968 I made a trip up to Oregon and Washington and had meetings in the various assemblies. It was good to visit the Fred Elliots in Portland; they were still grieving over their loss of Jim. It was a joy to see old friends from my Navy days in the area, my first visit since 1944. In June, Dorothy graduated and she also was granted two scholarships. That summer, too, Donna went with a group of young people to do evangelism in Quebec. She had been taking French and this gave her a practical exposure to the culture and the language. It was an exciting experience for her. We encouraged Dorothy to go on to college in the fall but she decided she wanted to move to Denver, to live with a friend and to be on her own. I took her to the bus station that fall and reluctantly said goodby. "I kissed her goodby and told her we loved her. The door was always open for her return. Marie wept and wept as they embraced."

I stopped to see Tom McCullagh on October 5 in Guthrie on my way east. He was dying of cancer. "Poor brother is very weak, has lost lots of blood. One wonders how long it will be. He wept as I talked to him. He said he so hated to be useless and a burden. He was ready to go, but he said Florence was not willing to give him up. Death is a terrible foe. I wept with him and longed for the day when there shall be no more death, every tear wiped away. As I left he insisted on giving me $10.00. He said, 'I will never preach again, but you can. This will be a little help.' He spoke of God's faithfulness. During one month

A DIFFICULT DECISION

while he was in the hospital over $6,000.00 came in and they could pay all bills. How wonderful." I left with a heavy heart; we had labored together in the gospel. His last words to me were, "Preach the gospel."

The next year, 1969, I taught again at Culver City in the spring. May 2 was my last day and I was surely discouraged with that class. "Any person who tries can pass my courses. However, many did not even turn in a term paper. As a result this really hit their grades. I had 17 fail in Christian Evidences and 12 in Doctrine. It was really sad. Those kids just goofed off. Most of them simply did not study. They went to movies, to the beach, listened to rock and roll, played games, etc. The culture of this area seems to be overpowering Christian testimony and distinctiveness." It was my last time to teach there. Later the school took a more liberal stance and finally died out.

Don Neilson and Donna were married in June. They had kept in touch since 1966 and the relationship had ripened into love and commitment. We were glad to see her marry a committed, earnest Christian. For the marriage we obtained the use of a church building in Camarillo and they asked me to perform the ceremony. It was a time of joy and rejoicing. After their honeymoon in Santa Barbara they went back to Colorado where Don was teaching school. Our family was growing up and scattering.

Donna was urging us to move further east for the sake of the boys. She said, "Papa, please move from California for the sake of the boys." During the 60s and 70s America went through the greatest societal change the country has ever known. And California led in the change. The pill was introduced and sex became divorced from marriage, commitment and children. Now sex was a form of recreation, open to all. The Beetles with their rock and roll popularized free sex, drugs and oriental religion. Moral absolutes were jettisoned and everything was permitted. We lived on what was called the "hippie flyway" with young people hitchhiking from L. A. to San Francisco. The Vietnam war was being protested and banks were being burned. It was a wild time and utterly bewildering to the older generation.

We felt our work with the assembly in Thousand Oaks was finished. A number of families were coming and two mature men were in leadership. The assembly in Santa Barbara pleaded with us to consider moving there to help them for a while. Las Cruces was urging us to consider moving there, as were Donna and Don in Greeley. But we had helped start the work in Santa Barbara years before but now it was largely made up of retired people. We finally decided to sell our house and we looked at a house in Greeley and one in Santa Barbara. The house in Greeley did not open up and that door seemed closed. The house in Santa Barbara did open up; they accepted the low bid we made. We moved to Santa Barbara in April, 1970. The assembly in Thousand Oaks had a lovely farewell for us and gave us leather bound "Hymns of Worship" and a generous gift of money. Farewells are always hard. But after our move our boys were very unhappy in Santa Barbara; there were no other young people there. What should we do?

13

COLORADO BOUND

In Santa Barbara we had a lovely home on the Mesa looking out over the Pacific Ocean. It was only a two block walk to the beach and my love for the sea was very strong. I loved to go down to the beach for my walk, breathing the invigorating tang of the salt air. Naturally speaking we did not want to move. But as we prayed about it, we felt we should investigate the possibility.

Frank Moffitt called us from Oklahoma City pleading with us to consider moving back to Oklahoma. The assembly was struggling because of some families having been transferred. Our daughter and son-in-law had moved to Greeley, Colorado, and were burdened to see an assembly established there. Don had graduated from the University there and was especially concerned for the students. He was urging us to come to help establish a work there. The California culture had not been good for our family and we felt a more central location would eliminate some of the driving I was having to do each year. And in April while still in Camarillo the doctor had said it seemed I was developing some asthma symptoms from the smog conditions.

After prayer we decided to put the house on the market and see if it would move. A realtor said to me, "Why do you want to move? I have traveled all over the world and there is no place I would rather live than here." Could not the Lord prevent the sale of the house if he wanted us to stay? We had seen the Lord stop the sale of our home in years past. The little assembly was urging us to stay and help build the work in Santa Barbara. Elmer Stone, an elder in the meeting, said, "This may be our last chance." And Marie was reluctant to move further away from her mother.

We had helped with the work at Verdugo Pines during the past four years, especially working with the high school camps. Numbers professed Christ each year and it was one of our more fruitful endeavors in California. 1969 was our last year there. We also had a good women's Bible class in Camarillo and a home Bible study at Gale O'Bryan's home in Saugus with some professing Christ. We had led Gale to the Lord some years before. The 1970 New Year's conference at Pomona had gone well. Roland Hill and I spoke with me taking up Titus.

In May 1970 I drove east for our Oklahoma camp, stopping for meetings in Tucson and also with the Liebs and the Odessa Christians. The little work in Odessa was just about finished, sad. Then it was on to Oklahoma City for meetings before the beginning of camp. That was such a good time, encouraging for the Christians and for me. We had decided to advertise the house while I was gone, asking a fairly high price for it. If it sold at that price we would take it that the Lord wanted us to move. The Saturday before camp Marie called to say that she had signed a contract. Apparently the house was sold. The die was cast and our indecision about moving was over. Now it was just a question of where to move.

The camp went well with Ben Parmer and Gordon Wakefield helping with the speaking. Don and Donna were also there to help but she had a miscarriage while there, a real disappointment for all of us. There were some twenty professions of salvation. After the camp I followed Don and Donna to Colorado and began house hunting in Greeley. I found one two blocks south of the campus with five bedrooms and a big fellowship room in the basement that would do well for meetings. They took my offer on it and I signed the contract.

I left the car in Colorado and flew home in time for Dan's graduation in the stadium in Camarillo. "It was a beautiful, clear evening. The mountains were beautiful. Dan looked handsome." Afterwards we had a Mexican dinner at El Tecolote, a happy evening tinged with the sorrow of leaving the area.

COLORADO BOUND

On June 20th I rented a U-haul truck and the boys and I loaded it with all of our belongings. It was completely packed. Later when it was weighed at a truck weight station they told us we had 12,740 pounds on board! We cleaned the house and left that evening to stay over night at Grandma Adams. Marie drove the station wagon and Dan rode with me. The highway skirts the sea from Santa Barbara to Ventura with the mountains for a back drop, striking scenery. "The coast was beautiful; the surf relentless in its attack on the beach. I love the sea and enjoyed the ride to the full. Beautiful, beautiful. As we left the sea at Ventura it was with real sadness." I was going to miss the ocean.

We spent the night at Grandma's and said goodby that night; we would leave early before she was awake. We prayed together that night; she was reluctant to see us leave. The parting was hard. The next morning we left at 4:00 a.m. to get on the road before the heat of the desert hit us. We made Needles by 11:00 a.m. and it was hot. Later that day it reached 115 degrees and there was no air conditioning in cars then. The truck was a little slow on the grades but we made Flagstaff that night and camped. The next day we stopped north of Santa Fe and the third day we made it to Greeley in time for supper with Donna and Don, very thankful for a safe trip.

Greeley is on the high plains at 4,700 feet with the mountains in view twenty miles to the west. It was a city then of about 35,000 people with the University of Northern Colorado, and surrounded by fertile, irrigated fields. In fact, our county is one of the most productive in the nation, agriculturally speaking. But it certainly wasn't scenic like Santa Barbara. However, we had peace in moving there and looked to the Lord for a time of rich blessing. The next day we unpacked the truck with the help of others. We put up the beds and left the rest in boxes because we had to leave quickly for Story Book Camp where I was to teach.

We had a good camp at Story Book and we were able to rest up a little after the past hectic days of moving. I took up the Life of Christ with the campers, a delightful study. We also stayed for junior camp as well. After camp we stopped in Willmar to revisit family. I was able to visit my Grandma in the hospital. She was 94 and coming to the end of life; I was able to pray with her. She could only moan in response. Grandma had a simple faith; as a child I can remember her praying in Norwegian. She had never learned English well. It was my last time to see her. Then it was home and the chore of unpacking and getting settled.

In August there were three camps at Camp Elim, near Colorado Springs, where I was the speaker. Our son-in-law Don directed one of the camps and it was a joy to work with him. He was young, enthusiastic and devoted to the Lord. They were good weeks with a number professing Christ.. Then it was back to Greeley to continue getting settled. Our boys started school after the Family Camp over Labor Day at Elim, where I took up First Epistle of John. Ken Baird and Marion Michaux also spoke.

That month Don had some car trouble and I helped him. "One day Don and I dropped his transmission and replaced the clutch. Quite the job; we finished about 11:30 p.m. at night. It was fun working with Don; he is a great guy. He has tremendous purpose, a single eye to glorify the Lord." We started having meetings in our large room in the basement, the "Underground Church!"

That October the Workers Conference was in Houston and I drove down, stopping in Oklahoma City for some meetings. Once again the dear saints there were pleading with us to move back to Oklahoma City but we were not going to move again very quickly.

The conference in Houston went well and I spent some extra time there with an old friend H.M.. He was quite taken with Jim McCotter and a movement he was heading called the "Blitz." Jim was a gifted evangelist and would take a team of young people to a university campus and do intensive evangelism. Then they would start their own house church. Herschel had moved near the university with a view to starting such a group. I deeply appreciated their evangelistic spirit but there were tendencies that bothered me. The Lord's soon return was stressed. In view of this, Jim urged young people to drop out of college, to live with others in a house in a commune setting, to work part time and to spend much time evangelizing. They saw souls saved but I felt they lacked balance. But I could see my friend was committed to Jim and he continued to work with him for years, leaving assembly fellowship.

The Blitz movement evolved through various stages. Jim controlled the groups with an iron hand. Groups were formed in a number of university cities and he appointed elders in every group, men who were fanatically loyal to him. He was viewed as the "apostle." At first I wanted to try to work with the groups and add a little age and experience. I had met Jim at Camp Elim at that college conference in 1966. But I soon discovered you did not work with Jim; you worked under him. If you crossed him you were disfellowshiped and shunned. Over the years the groups have formed another denomination called "Great Commission Churches" and function much like other churches with a pastoral staff. Jim was finally put out of the group, the details of which were hushed up. It saddened me to see the way things developed so that the movement was operating like a cult, with rigid mind control.

That fall Jim Wright had a number of weeks of intensive Bible study for serious young men and asked me to do some of the teaching. I spent several weeks at the camp teaching the Bible; a good time.

The work in Greeley was growing. We had a baptism the last of October in the lake at Glenmere Park for two students who had trusted Christ. A large crowd gathered around and heard the gospel. A cool wind was blowing but the fellowship and joy were warm. We began having the Sunday evening meal together at our home. This would be followed by singing and Bible study. The assembly in Littleton gave us twenty chairs, a real help for our seating. In December of 1970 we had a baptism for three: "The day was pleasant but the lake was cold with some ice on it. A good crowd gathered to hear the Gospel preached by Don. It was a time of real joy. We gave them a Christmas dinner at night and fed 53. Marie did a beautiful job."

People were being saved regularly and we had baptisms often. In the winter we often used a swimming pool in a health club. One fall, rather late, a student who was saved wanted to be baptized in a lake. We went out to Seeley Lake north of town and discovered a layer of ice on the lake! He insisted on being baptized anyway. We knocked a hole in the ice, baptized him, wrapped him in blankets and took him home for a hot shower. He survived with no ill effects. One winter day we had a baptism for Gordy, a quadriplegic who had trusted Christ. Four men carried him down into the water of the pool. We all sang and rejoiced with him and his wife. Dear Gordy! He has gone to be with the Lord now.

Besides intensive evangelism on campus and door-to-door work, a number of Bible studies were started in the dorms. Both Don and I were very active in this. For the believers I had various classes taking up books of the Bible, doctrine, church history and even Greek. It was enjoyable to get back into teaching Greek again. Our numbers were growing, about forty on Sunday mornings.

It was a time of great unrest among young people. Drug use was coming in and sex was most permissive. Anti Vietnam war rallies kept the campus in a turmoil. A P.A. system was set up on campus with an open mike for such rallies and our Christian students took the opportunity to proclaim their faith. It was a time of great excitement and many were being saved. We formed a student organization on campus and were able then to use rooms at the Student Center for films and studies. We also set up a book table on campus to distribute literature. During the summers I still worked in camps but much of the year I was busy locally. We also began a jail ministry as an assembly, going in regularly for Sunday services.

We also became interested in working with international students. A local organization called Friends of International Students assigned students to interested families. These then would show them hospitality and friendship. We became involved in 1970 and served on the board for many years in various capacities. Our first student was a girl from Iran named Soheila. She has viewed us as her American parents, calls us "Mom and Dad" and we still keep in touch.

Through the years we have had students from Iran, Saudi Arabia, Germany, Korea, Taiwan and China, with the most coming from Taiwan. We still keep in touch with many of these and have visited Taiwan twice to revisit our students, who treated us royally, paying our fare. As a group we sponsored a fall banquet, winter tea and spring farm tour. We have had many opportunities to share the gospel with all of the students and some have accepted Christ. We had a baptism up the Big Thompson Canyon and our Saudi Muslim student came along and heard the gospel again. It has been a happy, rewarding experience. At times we have had as many as 35 international students for a meal in our basement. Sad to say, community interest has ebbed and the organization ceased to exist in 2003. Individual families still work with students, however.

During the summer of 1972 I was invited to go to Colombia to speak at a missionary conference. Will Kinney who had been in our fellowship also went along with a view of staying in Latin America to do missionary work. I stayed with the Paul Gorings. It was a delightful time of teaching and fellowship with the various workers. I then flew to Ecuador and stayed with the Dick Farstads in Quito.

We rode the bus down to Shell in the jungle, a harrowing mountain ride, and then flew in to Arajuno, where Dick had served as a missionary. This was the departure point for the five who had been killed by the Waoranis (Aucas); it was a moving visit for me. I had known three of the men. It was a great joy to fellowship with the native believers there. "The jungle is beautiful, green and full of life, including chiggers! The Arajuno River roared just below my bedroom window, a lovely view." I also visited Frank Kollinger at Chama, another outpost. Then it was back up the mountains on a bus to Quito. We also visited assemblies in Quito. From there I flew home.

As our numbers grew we simply did not have enough room in our basement. A house that had been used for student work by the Methodist Church went on the market. It was right across from the campus and had a large living room and dining room area. The Methodists had been renting it to students and now were anxious to sell it. The house had been neglected and was filthy dirty. Students had kept big dogs in the house and it was known for drug use. We made a low bid of $29,000.00 and they took it. The deal was completed in September, 1972. The Lord had provided us with a better place for meetings and also a place where Christian students could live. We all went to work, cleaning it up and painting it.

We decided to name it the Koinonia House (Greek for fellowship). We put up an attractive sign in front that read "The Truth Is In Jesus." We were right across from the administration building and all could read it. This aroused the ire of the radical campus newspaper. They published cartoons and editorials ridiculing our position. If only we had stated "Some Truth Is In Jesus," it would have been acceptable. New Age thinking can accept that. But to say that Jesus is the only way to spiritual truth and God was deemed the height of ignorance by them. At that time we had the largest student work of any church in town and were known around the campus.

The Lord continued to bless. We did extensive door-to-door work in town. One time we covered a number of churches which did not preach the gospel with tracts as members were exiting their services. This created quite a stir! Our folk were very bold in evangelizing. We also went over to Fort Collins, Rock Springs and Laramie as a group to evangelize there.

In May 1973 we had a baptism for six, among them Marty. Marty had been very depressed and suicidal, her life a mess. She accepted the Lord and began to meet with us. The Lord was healing her mind and soul. Her father, a professor at the University said, "We had tried everything, counselors, various programs and psychiatrists. Your fellowship has helped her when nothing else could." I have heard her pray, "Thank you, Lord, for healing me." Thank God for the power of the gospel.

That summer I was asked to help with the teaching of teams of young people doing evangelism in Europe. Don and Donna wanted to come along. We left from Toronto, after our camp in Oklahoma, on a charter flight for Belgium. We stayed at St. Joseph's Seminary in Mechelin for an orientation week. Then the teams scattered to various parts of Europe. We visited various teams in Austria and Italy, having times of intensive teaching with them. It was an exciting time. They were zealous young people from a number of countries around the world. They did tract work, sold books and had evangelistic meetings. We were given the use of a VW for the summer and drove thousands of kilometers.

In 1974 we sent a team of seven men up to Laramie to live and to start a work there. I went up with them and we located a house for them to rent. They settled in, got jobs and began to reach out. Steve Carr was a good evangelist and did preaching on the campus of the University of Wyoming. Some were saved, among them Pat Woodward, who has been a missionary in Europe for some years. I would drive up every two weeks for Bible studies and Greek. Some of them wanted to take Greek and I was glad for the opportunity. But in the winter the road conditions could be wild, with fierce ground blizzards creating white-out conditions. There were many times when I prayed earnestly that I would get home safely! But the little group needed encouragement. They said, "We would have quit if you had not come up regularly."

In 1975 I was asked to return to teach again in Europe and this time Marie went along. We spent most of our time in Troyes, France, with a team there. I drove an old diesel truck, hauling team supplies. Troyes was a picturesque city of 120,000 people but with very few Christians. A Christian engineer named Pierre Kislig wanted to see a testimony begun there; we stayed in their apartment, lovely people. I wrote: "Pierre is convinced of New Testament principles so we are most compatible. Praise the Lord!"

It was a time of daily Bible teaching and intensive evangelism. Bernard was the enthusiastic team leader and did very well. The young people were hungry for teaching. One girl told us she was the only Christian in her town. Patricia, a girl from England, was my interpreter, although a number knew English. We would put up posters announcing our evening meetings. Then the communists would come through and plaster their slogans over ours. We would go back and put ours up again. This went on several times—a real propaganda war. The good news is that a church is going on there today and one of the families in the fellowship first heard the gospel in our street meetings. It was with real sorrow that we said goodby to the members of that team.

We had train passes and visited some of my family members in Stavanger, Norway, before returning home. There was opportunity to witness and we discovered that some of them knew the Lord. It was a trip I had longed to take all of my life. My grandparents had come from there and I had heard of the beauty of Norway, its fjords and mountains. It was all true! From there we went to Vienna, Austria, and spent some time with a team there and visited friends from my previous visit. We went with the team for a street meeting; I spoke by translation, an exciting time.

Then it was on to Italy to visit the Lord's work in Florence and Rome, where Dan Pasquale picked us up. I did some teaching with the team doing outreach there. Sam Lindsay from Ireland was working with a team in Pisa and we visited them also. We had worked with Sam before in Italy, a dear brother. Then it was on to Vichy, France, and some time with Trifon and Priscilla Kaliodjoglou and the assembly there. Finally we arrived back in Belgium and caught the charter flight back to New York.

It was good to be back with our assembly and to share with them the blessings of our trip. The work had gone on well in our absence and we were excited about the outreach for the fall.

The Workers' Conference that October was in Saint Louis at Maplewood and went well. It was a tremendous time of encouragement and fellowship.

But tragedy was about to strike our family. At 2:00 a.m. on October 22, 1975 I received a call from the hospital. Our oldest son Dan had been in a car accident and we needed to come to the hospital immediately. At first doctors thought his injury was not too serious but as time went on paralysis set in and they transferred him to a hospital in Denver for surgery. The surgery did not help; the spinal cord was severed. Dan would be a paraplegic for the rest of his life. I wrote: "These last days have been some of the most terrible in our lives." Later I wrote a book on the tragedy of his life entitled *Danny, A Life Cut Short*. He had a massive heart attack in 1981 and died. It has been a great sorrow of our life. We have a tremendous sense of loss; he was our eldest son. But life has to go on and the Lord gives grace.

15

A Death and Rebirth

The work at the chapel continued with the Lord's blessing. We saw some turning to Christ regularly and being added to the fellowhip. Because we had a strong student work we would lose some every year as they graduated and moved on. Today there are Christians scattered across the country who first came to Christ here.

The first part of June 1975 we had sent two teams of six students to Wyoming to do outreach, one to Rock Springs and one to Laramie. We had some contacts in Rock Springs and there was the new small assembly in Laramie which had begun the year before. It was an encouraging time.

In March of 1976 I was asked to take a funeral. Bob had a sister named Billie who had been saved and was in our fellowship. The previous Friday he had called his mother and sister to say he was going to take his life. He had been on drugs and alcohol and was very depressed. His mother urged him to turn to God. He said, "I don't believe in God." She pleaded earnestly with him but he would not listen. His mother was called Saturday morning by the police in Chicago. Bob had jumped from the 96th floor of the John Hancock building. They shipped his mangled body to Greeley for burial and we had the service. His mother said to me, "I suppose he is in hell." What could one say to her? I could only preach the gospel at the service and pray that the living would lay it to heart. His father stood and looked at the casket for a long time with a broken heart after the others had gone. He was not a believer and had no hope either.

After camps in the summer I went to Regent College in Vancouver for a summer session, the last of July. F. F. Bruce was teaching on Jesus and the Gospels; I had enjoyed his writings for years and wanted to study under him. I also took a class with John Yoder on New Testament Ethics. It was intellectually and spiritually stimulating. The men and women there were mature and intelligent, a challenging environment. I was also able to spend time with Dex Sederstrom in Seattle, an old friend. F. F. Bruce had a phenomenal memory. He was the editor of the *Evangelical Quarterly* and had published some of my writing. When he met me, he said, "Oh yes, I remember you from your writing!" I took a picture of him and his wife and sent them a copy. He said it was the best picture he had ever had taken and used it in his autobiography. He was a gifted, godly man, an elder in his assembly in England. As we parted, he said, "I hope we will keep in touch."

A brother from our assembly, Trip Moore, was concerned for Quebec and moved to Quebec City. I visited him in September 1976 and spent some days with him and several others who desired to begin a work there. Quebec was then very weak as far as evangelical Christianity is concerned. We looked for an apartment for Don and our daughter Donna who were concerned to move there and help the work.

We had a happy family Thanksgiving together that year with Don and Donna and others. They were packing to leave for Quebec planning to work with Trip Moore in the establishing of an assembly. French Quebec was, and is, very, very needy for the gospel. They said goodby to the saints on Nov. 28 after a special meeting. "It was moving to see Don and Donna being embraced as the tears flowed. They are much loved."

We had worked together for six years and had seen much blessing. We made a good team, different in gift and personality. We would miss them dearly. "Then the parting—our hardest yet. Tears flowed and we embraced fervently. Donna clung to me sobbing, Don too—I felt so close to him. We have had our differences; both of us are strong minded. But the Lord has given grace and I love him and appreciate him now more than ever. It is like an amputation and there is a deep, hollow ache. We will greatly miss them and Mark, dear little guy, our only grandchild."

Dissent was brewing in the assembly. Some of the women were reading books on the "Christian women's lib" movement. Virginia Ramey Mollenkot was a leader in that movement, advocating an egalitarian position, no difference in the roles of the sexes. She later began defending homosexuality, then became apostate, divorced her husband and became a lesbian. But her writings then and that of others were popular in some Christian circles. The talk and criticism was going on for some time before we were aware of it. There was also talk of rejecting leadership by elders and making decisions by consensus of the whole group. Because of my stand on these matters my family and I came under strong attack.

In February 1977 the attacks became vicious. It was especially hard for us. These were people we had helped lead to the Lord and had taught. They were our spiritual children. Satan was creating utter confusion and suspicion. One woman was a leader in influencing the women against us. We had worked closely with her, teaching her and helping her. We also married her and her husband. We had worked closely together. She wanted to start a Bible class in a women's dorm but felt inadequate. She asked me to teach her the passage and then she would teach it to the girls. A number were saved out of that study.

Now she and her husband were undermining the work. Years later she came to us in tears, asking for forgiveness for what she had done. But the damage was done. She and her husband finally withdrew from the fellowship and went to another church. After their leaving, the dissension quieted down somewhat, but there was still an undercurrent. Some were defending us and our position; others were attacking us.

During April I flew to Toronto for a conference. It was large; about 800 were present. Peter Pell, James Gunn, David Ward and I were the speakers. It was a great time of teaching and fellowship. From there I went to Quebec City for some time with Don and Donna and the small group meeting with them. It was so good to see them again and little Mark. It has also been a joy to visit Jean Paul Berney on my trips to Quebec and to see the good work he has been doing. He has been a faithful servant of the Lord through the years.

Several younger men had worked with Don and me in leadership. One of them named Bob continued his attacks on us. Finally the others read a statement the last of April affirming their support of us in leadership. We hoped that would settle the matter, but the attacks continued. The Scripture warns, *"looking carefully lest anyone fall short of the grace of God, lest any root of bitterness springing up cause trouble, and by this many become defiled"* (Heb. 12:15). Many were becoming defiled. The tension was beginning to affect our health; Marie's blood pressure was too high. I began to struggle with bitterness myself over the injustice of it all.

For some time we had been going over to Sterling, Colorado, for regular Bible studies and hoped to see a work begun there. Some were saved and showed interest. During May I had a week of meetings with them. Bob and Cheryl Hunter accompanied me and helped with the series.

If we had not had trouble in our own assembly we might have seen more done there. That June we had our 20th year at Sooner Bible Camp and a great camp with twelve professing Christ. We also had a good camp later at Story Book in cool, northern Minnesota.

Roman Romero stayed in our home while we were gone. Roman had come to the university from a Catholic monastery, was saved and came into our fellowship. He was one of our spiritual sons, now with the Lord. Aug. 2nd a group of us from our fellowship climbed Long's Peak, a beautiful day, always an awesome experience. Aug. 17 Jim Simons and I spent a week visiting the fellowships in Laramie and Rock Springs for teaching and encouragement. Then later in August, Don, Donna and Mark left for Quebec after a lengthy visit in Colorado.

The bitterness against us was escalating. I was accused of being inflexible because of my stand on the role of women and leadership by elders. They felt all decisions should be made by consensus of the whole fellowship. There was talk by them of putting me out of leadership. I decided to do nothing until after the Workers' Conference which was held in Minneapolis the first week of October.

When we returned these young leaders wanted to discipline me for my doctrinal stand. Finally on October 9 an afternoon meeting was called of all the men. Some were unaware of the full extent of the strife which had been going on in the leadership. Bitter, harsh things were said at that meeting. I was compared to "a cancer which must be cut out for the health of the body!" This was a man I had discipled and had married him and his wife. When I refused to accept their discipline of excommunication they walked out in anger. "I called for the rest to wait and pray. We held hands and I prayed, thanking God for a coming day when we shall be with the Lord and like Him." "I drove home feeling just numb—the emotional trauma is fierce. But at least the fellowship knows what the issues are."

"This has been the most distressing eight months in the Lord's work we have ever known. Part of today I have just wept. It is all so sad. We have had such a sense of rejection and failure at times." The next few Sundays Marie and I decided to visit other assemblies. We heard later that the next Sunday after the Lord's Supper they conducted an accusation session against me. They "put the whole weight of blame on me for frustrating their desires for change—place of women, etc. The Lord knows how it will end."

After several other talks with those opposing us it was obvious there could be no reconciliation. Finally on November 6 we began meeting separately and they moved out of the Koinonia House. Two older men, Marino Montoya and Fred Hover, were committed to meeting with us and there were some others as well. But when there is trouble many are confused, just wanting peace. Roman said, *"Smite the shepherd and the sheep are scattered."* Some left to join other churches and some decided to stay together and to rent a store front for meetings. And so with a heavy heart we saw the work divided, seven years of labor destroyed. We lost twenty two couples and fifteen or twenty singles. It was a mortal wound to us. The other group met for some months and then that work died. People who left them told us, "We were not being fed nor shepherded."

We struggled on for some years with a handful. Church trouble leaves a stench in a community. We still did our camp work in the summer and jail work through the year. We also did some campus work and carried on our work with international students. Finally it was decided to sell the Koinonia House and to buy a used church building that had come up for sale. This would give us more room for a Sunday School and be more suited for families. We had bought the house in 1972 and sold it in 1985. We called our new building Fellowship Chapel; it was at 1203 12th Avenue.

Since we were so small it was decided to go to the assembly in Fort Collins for a while to encourage them. We continued our night Bible studies at our chapel. In Fort Collins they were going through struggles also and we thought we could help them. We did see two new families come into the fellowship there. But Pentecostal teaching was coming in and the assembly had been taught to put the older men out of leadership and to put in young men. This they did and the younger leaders really did not want any help. One of the deacons told me, "Our leaders do not know what they believe and are afraid to take a stand on anything." After two years we decided we could not help them and restarted our meetings in Greeley. Some time later their young leadership decided to shut down the work and sell the building. I had worked some with that assembly in the early years helping them get started. And now the work was scattered. It is a serious matter to destroy a temple of God (1 Cor. 3:16-17[2]).

We had two young couples that we had seen come to the Lord who wanted to restart our meetings in Greeley. We told them, "It will be hard, but if you are committed God will bless and the work will grow." We were just six adults and two small children as we began again to break bread together in 1989. It is very hard to begin a work with such a small group. To others coming in it looks as if the work is so weak that it will surely die. A crowd tends to attract a crowd. But one advantage is that

---

[2] Know ye not that ye are the temple of God, and that the Spirit of God dwelleth in you? If any man defile the temple of God, him shall God destroy; for the temple of God is holy, which temple ye are.

A DEATH AND REBIRTH

smallness encourages participation. One of our men said to me, "Now don't expect me to speak!" But as time went by both men began to take more and more part and both are good teachers of the Word today.

A man who has climbed Long's Peak many times was asked for advice in climbing the 14,256 foot peak. He said, "Persevere!" It is fifteen, grueling miles. That is good advice in the Lord's work too. Leonard Lindsted told me years ago, "Don, I have thought of quitting a thousand times, but I am no quitter!" To which I could say, "Amen!" And so we have persevered and the Lord has gradually built the work. We continued with the jail work and probably have more converted felons meeting with us than most assemblies. We have done door-to-door work and worked with international students. We began Fellowship Family Camp in 1994 and rent a campground near Estes Park in the shadow of Long's Peak, a magnificent setting surrounded by lofty mountains.

Our church building had steep stairs leading up to the chapel and no parking lot. We had a brother in a wheel chair and men had to carry him up the stairs. Others had trouble climbing the stairs. We decided to look for a different building and located one at 2100 22nd Street. It had a chapel that would seat about 150 with good access and adequate parking. It had not been used for a year and looked very neglected, but it was a solid brick building. It had been built by the Jehovah's Witnesses originally. A Baptist church tried to start a work there later but had trouble and the preacher left. They were desperate to sell and pay off their mortgage.

A realtor had a contract on it with a view to tear it down and build apartments. We decided to put a back-up contract on it contingent upon the sale of our building. Then we waited and prayed. The neighbors rose up in arms over the idea of apartments and wanted to keep a church there instead. So the zoning board denied his request. Now we had to sell our building. It sold almost immediately for our asking price! As we closed the deal on our new building in May 2001 the realtor said, "God must have wanted you to have this building!" To which we could say, "Amen!" We bought our new chapel for $20,000 less than we were given for our old chapel.

One thing this new chapel lacked was a dining room and kitchen. We promised the ladies we would build on to the present building. This we finished in 2003 and the ladies were delighted. We have fellowship meals together quite often and the addition meets that need. We did not need to go in debt on the building for which we are most thankful.

While we were so small I spent most of my time with the local work. I have never traveled to augment my income. The Lord has been faithful and met our every need. I could write a book about that alone. In more recent years I have traveled more in conference work and in teaching overseas. Trips have been made to Europe, S. Korea, Japan and Taiwan. I was asked to teach in a Bible school being started by assemblies in Korea and for several years spent two or three weeks at a time teaching there. It has been a delightful experience. We had a Korean student live with us for two years while he finished his PhD and have many friends in the Far East.

We pray that this work for God may continue as a witness to His love and grace until the Lord Himself returns.

Don Neilson family 1977

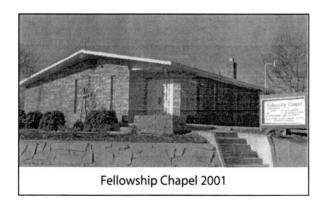
Fellowship Chapel 2001

LIFE IS A MOUNTAIN

Norbies March 21, 1997

Appendix 1

Life Is A Mountain

I grew up in Arizona in Prescott and Tucson where mountains were always near. As a young man with some other young men we climbed Mount Baldy, which is south of Tucson. It was rather a long hike and I still remember the excitement of reaching the top and talking to the fire lookout who was stationed there. It was so delightful to be up in the pines, high above the arid heat of the desert. And I also went up Mt. Lemon which is north of Tucson. To get to it you had to take a one-way road from Oracle up the mountain, which was an adventure in itself; and then there were the lower desert mountains which we hiked.

But then after my Navy and college days we lived in the Midwest where we had hills but no real mountains. In California we lived near the lower mountains along the coast. However, it was when we moved to Colorado in 1970 that I was once again near the high mountains. Twenty miles to the west of us the Rocky Mountains begin and we soon fell in love with them. Long's Peak was about fifty miles west of us and could be clearly seen, the highest peak in N. Colorado at 14, 256 feet. It towers over the many other peaks in Rocky Mountain National Park, one of the most spectacular parks in the U. S. From time to time we have camped there and hiked the various trails. It is close enough that we can go up for a day outing. The mountains have given us much joy and can be therapeutic, calming the soul and removing the cares of life. Often while hiking the Lord has given me a message or poem and times to pray.

LIFE IS A MOUNTAIN

The first time I went up Long's Peak was September 1, 1971. Marie and our sons, Doug and Dale, went along. We left the Ranger Station at 5:45 a.m. and it turned out to be a harder climb than we anticipated. It is about seven and a half miles each way with an elevation gain of about 5,000 feet. We went up the North Face and Marie waited at the Boulder Field; she was utterly exhausted. I had waited for her so I was late but finally made the summit at 2:10 a.m., which is too late to be on top but the Lord gave us good weather. The summit is flat, about the size of a football field, with magnificent views. The horizon there is 120 miles so one can see up into Wyoming and south to Pike's Peak. The east face has a sheer cliff of about 2,000 feet. It is a great place to eat lunch! Then there is the long climb down, past the Homestretch, the Narrows, the Trough, the Ledges and finally the Boulder Field and the trail. The boys and I made it to the top and we were very tired coming down. We finally made the Ranger Station at 7:40 p.m..

It became my favorite mountain and because of its proximity, one that I climbed more often than any other—25 times to the top. I climbed the North Face and once the East Face, a challenging, technical climb. Two other times I was turned back on the Narrows by severe weather. One has to know when to turn back. The mountain can be very unforgiving of mistakes. Nearly every year someone dies on that mountain. They say that if you can climb Long's you can climb any mountain in Colorado, although some are more dangerous.

I have climbed other mountains in the state. There are 54 over 14, 000 feet, more high mountains than any other of the 48 states. Bill Lansdown, a dear friend from Kansas Bible Camp days and I have climbed a number. My son, Doug and I have climbed some and others have gone with me too. Some of the easier ones I have climbed alone but that can be risky. So much depends on the weather. Some I have not climbed because they are only accessible with a four wheel drive vehicle. Here are the 39 over 14, 000 feet that I have climbed, some of them several times: Mt. Elbert, Uncompagre Peak, Castle Peak, Mt. Princeton, Mt. Massive, Mt. Lincoln, Mt. Evans, Mt. Belford, Mt Harvard, Gray's Peak, Quandary Peak, Mt. Yale,

APPENDIX 1: LIFE IS A MOUNTAIN

Blanca Peak, Mt. Antero, Long's Peak, Crestone Needle, La Plata Peak, Torrey's Peak, Mt. Shavano, Mt. Bross, Tabeguache, Mt. Columbia, Mt. Sherman, Huron Peak, Mt. Oxford, Missouri Mt., Red Cloud Peak, Mt. of the Holy Cross, Mt. Sneffels, Humboldt Peak, Wilson Peak, Sunshine Peak, Mt. Democrat, Mt. Bierstadt, Matterhorn Peak, Ellingwood Peak, Pike's Peak, Handes Peak, San Luis Peak.

I did not start climbing these until I was 49, a little late. I never climbed on the week end because of the Lord's Day. It has never been the obsession that grips some climbers but a nice hobby that stresses one physically and is exhilarating and humbling, a spiritual experience. Bill and I used to stand on a summit and sing, "Praise the Saviour, ye who know Him." Yes, it is grand to know the One who created it all. Anyone who climbs a lot may encounter some dangerous experiences. Here are a few of mine.

Long's Peak

The middle of August 1972 Bill and I tried to climb Long's Peak but were turned back by heavy snow at Jim's Grove. It snowed eight inches! The next week, August 31, a college student named Ron and I tried it again. We left at 5:45 a.m. and made good time. But as we started to climb the North Face the weather looked ominous. I thought we should turn back but Ron desperately wanted to climb that mountain. So I gave in but the storm hit us as we were climbing. There was howling wind, driving snow, thunder and lightning. The air was electric, making one's hair stand up. We could not turn back and there was no shelter from the storm. We were praying fervently as we struggled up the mountain. We made the summit at 11:30 a.m.; the storm passed on and the sun came out.

Ron and I gave thanks to God and started our descent. The homestretch is composed of steep slabs of rock, a challenge when dry, but very hazardous when covered with snow. As we descended, the snow began to melt and the descent went well. We met a couple coming up; they had waited out the storm in the hut at the Boulder Field. We reached our car at 5:45 p.m., very thankful. It was my introduction to storms on a 14,000 foot peak, a terrifying experience. This storm moved in earlier than usual and caught us.

I had climbed Longs many times using the Keyhole route or the North Face. I had often looked at the magnificent East Face from Chasm Lake, which is nestled at its base. It is described as the most magnificent cirque in the Rockies. I decided before I was any older to climb it. It is a technical climb and I enlisted the help of a man who worked for a climbing school, he had the equipment and had climbed the East Face. I had done a little technical climbing before.

We left the Ranger Station on July 29, 1986, at 2:37 a.m. for an early start. Beyond Chasm Lake we put on crampons and used our ice axes as we ascended Mill's Glacier and Lamb's Slide, a steep snow and ice field. Because it was so icy it made for slow going. But we made it to the Broadway, a narrow shelf that cuts across the cliff, by 8:15 a.m. We took off our crampons and rested. That ice field was tiring. It was a clear day with a splendid sunrise and the view was magnificent, stretching away to the plains to the east. Hayner was the lead man, putting in protection and I anchored him; pitch by pitch working our way up the mountain. We were taking Kiener's Route, a classic climb. We worked our way along Broadway, then climbed up the Notch Couloir toward the Notch and then along the Diamond to the summit at 12:30 p.m.

We sat there, eating our lunch with a sense of triumph. We had made it and we felt a real sense of affection for the old mountain. What a magnificent, awesome mountain it is! After lunch we rappelled off the North Face, the quick way to come down. Then we hiked to the Boulder Field and picked up the trail. From there it was six weary miles but with a deep sense of satisfaction, We made the Ranger Station at 5:35 p.m., a long day. The Lord had given us good weather and we had made it. Long's Peak has been my favorite mountain.

A Challenge

The peak looms,
Tall, dark, strong,
Massive brow cloud-wreathed,
Features rough-hewn,
Fresh from the Master's hand,
As yet unsmoothed
By Nature's gentler touch.
Unknown, mysterious, difficult,
A challenge to be climbed,
A test of skill, nerve and endurance.
Fingers and toes clutch eagerly
At rocky wrinkles,
Heart pounding, lungs gasping for air.
Muscles cry out from strain
As nerves are rubbed raw by danger.
A final struggle,
The crest is reached.
The view immense, self-shrinking,
The steep ascent now understood,
As I sit perched
By the side of God.
Life is a mountain to be climbed,
Unknown, mysterious, difficult. . . .

Donald L. Norbie
December 11, 1972
(Long's Peak)

Mount of the Holy Cross

Bill and I planned to climb Mount of the Holy Cross on August 17, 1979. But his plans changed and he could not make it. Marie and I camped at the trail head at Half Moon Campground and I decided to climb it solo, trusting there would be some others making the climb too. At times when the snow lies right a cross can be seen on the mountain. I left our camp at 6:00 a.m. and moved along. You climb to Half Moon Pass at 11,600 feet and then drop 900' feet into a valley and then start up again. Above tree line the weather was not looking good at 10:00 a.m. Two younger men passed me, driving hard for the summit. I decided to follow them and made the summit at 1:15 p.m..

We started down at 1:30 p.m., but the storm moved in with zero visibility, sleet and icy rain. A little above tree line I lost them; they were moving rapidly. The rocks were getting icy and slick. I took a bad tumble and realized I had hurt my ankle. I thought it was sprained but it would flop over. I sat down and took out an ace bandage that I always carry. I wrapped the ankle tightly and then I could walk on it with pain. I hobbled down the trail to a deserted, abandoned cabin in the valley. Two hikers were going to spend the night there and they encouraged me to do that. But I knew Marie would be worried. They gave me hot chocolate and I pressed on. I cut down a small spruce tree to make a staff and started up to the Pass 900 feet above. It was 6:00 p.m. and I still had four miles to go. It was raining and I was getting cold, wet and hurting.

I reached the car at 7:35 p.m., cold, wet and exhausted, but very thankful to have made it. I changed clothes, ate, crawled into my sleeping bag and went to sleep. In the morning my ankle was very swollen. We broke camp and I drove out to the highway where Marie began to drive. (It is seven miles to the summit with a gain of 4,500' plus the 900' on the return, a real killer.) At home we went to see an orthopedic doctor who told us it was not a sprain, but a fractured ankle with badly torn ligaments. He asked how far I had walked out on it. When I said it was six miles, he said, You must have been biting a bullet with each step!" The good news is that it healed well and I continued my climbing. The Lord is good.

APPENDIX 1: LIFE IS A MOUNTAIN

Tabeguache Mountain

Bruce and I climbed Tabeguache on September 11, 1984. There was a terrible road going in; we should have had a jeep. Bruce had to push at times to keep us moving. We camped about half a mile from the trail head. We were up early and left the trail head at 5:15 a.m.. We made good time and reached a sub peak at 7:33 a.m. (13,100 feet). The clouds were beginning to come in and it was not looking good. However it was early and we decided to press on. We reached the summit at 9:28 a.m. and began the descent immediately. The clouds were rolling in.

A blizzard hit us as we started down. There were high winds 50-60 mph with sleet, snow and rain. Bruce had a jacket and rain pants; I had only a poncho. I had tried to get rain pants before the hike but the store was sold out. My old ones had worn out. At the trail head there was a sign warning not to take the wrong ridge and go down McCoy Gulch. People had ended up in big trouble going that way. We were working our way down, Bruce in the lead, fighting the wind and snow. Visibility was very low with white out conditions. Bruce shouted, "Here's where we go down the ridge." I felt a little uneasy, thinking it was too soon. I asked him, "Are you sure?" He said, "I am sure." The storm was getting more fierce and my legs were wet and cold. After we had gone down the ridge for some distance, the storm lifted for a minute and I realized we were on the wrong ridge. The storm closed in again and I got out my compass to get oriented. Then we had to retrace our steps, a dangerous loss of time.

I began to suffer from hypothermia. By the time we got back to the main ridge my teeth were chattering; my speech was becoming slurred. Bruce noticed that my eyes were not focusing normally and were glazing. I saw fear in his eyes. At that moment I think we both knew that we might die up there. "But we had prayed and I had peace, no fear. Bruce steadied me and we staggered along the ridge." I was stumbling at times, but we had to keep moving. We had no idea how long the storm would last.

"Around 13,200 feet I lost vision, could see nothing but a blue light. I said to Bruce, 'I can't see at all.' He took me by the hand and talked me down the mountain, step by step, from boulder to boulder, very loving and patient. At 3,000 feet the storm ceased after the saddle. The sun came out and we slowly made our way down to the trail head. It took us 4 hours and 15 minutes to reach the summit; 9 hours and 30 minutes to return. We were two thankful men when we reached the car at about 7 p.m. We broke camp and Bruce started driving. My sight was beginning to return when we reached Leadville. Bruce was tired and I was able to drive as we neared Denver. We were home by 2:40 a.m. I never climbed again without rain pants! We felt the Lord's presence and protection, and a sense of His peace.

Appendix 2

In Journeys Often

During His ministry Jesus chose His twelve apostles. *"Then He appointed twelve that they might be with Him and that He might send them out to preach"* (Mark 3:14 NKJV). In His ministry Christ traveled from village to village, from town to town. And His apostles followed His example. Paul spoke of *"journeys often."* (2 Cor. 11:26) and this was the pattern of the early workers. Paul might stay for periods of time in a certain city and then he would travel on to help other areas too. His ministry was wider than one local church. This caused local elders to take responsibility and to develop their gifts.

My wife and I have helped with the beginning of several local assemblies. In the beginning of such, one must spend much time locally, teaching and training young believers. But as a work matures one feels free to travel to help other groups. There are many small assemblies that need encouragement. Some workers are more gifted in evangelism and others in teaching. Both gifts are needed in the building up of God's people. Each worker is the Lord's bond servant (Gal. 1:10[3]) and should be alert to His leading as to the place of service and the content of the message. It is always gratifying to hear the Lord's people say after a meeting, "That is just what we needed!" One should never travel because finances are slim. God is able to supply your needs where you are. Pioneer work requires faith.

---

3 For do I now persuade men, or God? or do I seek to please men? for if I yet pleased men, I should not be the servant of Christ.

In early years our travels were more limited to the United States and Canada, with most of my time being spent in the Midwest and Southwest. There were some visits to Mexico in the 1950's and 60s to Chihuahua and the Baja. Then after we moved to Colorado in 1970 I was invited to speak at a missionary conference in Medellin, Colombia in 1972. This was a challenging time and I was happy to see some workers that we had known in years past: the Lehmans, Gorings and Duckhorns. I also went down to Ecuador and spent time with Dick and Jane Farstad, former students from Emmaus days. Some time was spent in Quito and also in the jungle. After speaking at a conference in Shell, I also visited Arajuno, a moving experience, rich with memories of the five who were speared to death by the Waorani (Aucas). Dick and I visited a family across the river, taking a dugout canoe to the other side. Apparently I picked up amoebic dysentery in Guayaquil and struggled with this for some time.

In 1973 I was invited to spend the summer in Europe teaching teams of young people doing evangelism. My son-in-law Don Neilson and Donna went along and we had a most interesting summer, spending most of our time in cities and towns in Austria and Italy. It was an exhausting but rewarding time. These were keen young people from the States, Canada and various countries of Europe.

Then in 1975 my wife and I went to Europe and engaged in the same teaching ministry, but this time we stayed mostly with one team in Troyes, France. They were great young people from ten different countries and we are still in touch with some of them. We also spent time in Austria and Italy, with a trip to Norway at the end where my ancestors were deeply rooted. Beautiful Norway with its sea, fjords and majestic mountains. I can understand why my grandparents in Minnesota missed Norway.

We had a bad hailstorm that ruined our roof. I roofed it myself and saved the insurance money. Marie said to me, "You have always wanted to go to Israel. Why don't you go on a tour?" We checked prices but it was a little too expensive for her to go with me. I decided we would just go on our own and bought a book entitled "Israel on $15.00 a day." It told how to economize, the names of cheap hotels and hostels and inexpensive restaurants. We went when in November 1979 prices were low.

We flew into Tel Aviv and caught a group taxi to Jerusalem. We went through a thunderstorm on our way up to the city, an exciting entry into that ancient city. We went to the old city, looked around and rented a room in what had once been a Catholic seminary. We had no time constraints and worked out our own itinerary. With a bus pass we were able to travel throughout the land inexpensively and made Jerusalem our base. This was before the terrorism began and we felt quite safe. It was great to visit Bethlehem and the House of Hope, where blind and handicapped Arabs are cared for in a loving way. It was a privilege to spend time with May Lada, a blind lady who had helped begin this faith work. The work continues today, carried on by Rhoda David and her helpers.

We were able to spend time in Nazareth staying in the home of Jamiel Basha, a godly elder in the assembly. We could stand on the roof of his house and see Mt. Lebanon and Mt. Gilboa. These Biblical sites became alive to us as we visited them, not just a name but a fascinating, historic place with deep roots in antiquity. It was such a joy to teach and to fellowship with the dear believers there. Jamiel told me when he visited London, customs asked him what he did; he said he was a carpenter. They announced excitedly over the P.A., "We have a carpenter from Nazareth here!"

We rode the buses from Dan to Beersheba, visiting Biblical sites along the way. We visited Qumran, the site of the Dead Sea scrolls. While there we encountered a tour group of Mormon missionaries who invited us to continue the tour that day with them. It meant we would not have to wait for our bus. We accepted and went with them to En Gedi, Masada, Arad and then back to Jerusalem. They tried to convert us and we did the same, leaving them tracts. Neither of us succeeded in converting the other! Masada was a moving experience. It was Herod's fortified palace on a steep, rocky bluff, made sacred to the Jews because of the band of Jews who died there opposing Rome in 132 A. D.

LIFE IS A MOUNTAIN

Before leaving for home we decided to ride the bus to Eilat on the Red Sea. Men with rooms to rent would meet people getting off the bus. A Jewish man said, "Look at the room; if you don't like it I will bring you back." It was a small house with several bedrooms and renters shared the kitchen. It was spartan—but cheap. That evening we reserved seats on a tour bus going down to Mt. Sinai and the St. Catharines monastery. We left very early on a rough road through the desert. The area had just been turned back to Egypt and we had to clear their check point. It is beautiful country in a raw, arid way.

We arrived safely and spent some hours under the shadow of Mt. Sinai or Jebel Musa (7,370'), that rugged, awesome mountain. It was a fitting setting for the giving of the Ten Commandments, God's holy standard. It was interesting to have a tour of the monastery, one of the most ancient belonging to the Orthodox Church. It was here that Tischendorf discovered the Codex Sinaiticus, a valued manuscript of the Scripture dating back to the fourth century. The library still has many ancient volumes. There is a valley at the base of the mountain about four miles long and one mile wide, adequate room for Israel's encampment. And four streams besides springs and wells supply adequate water for such a multitude.

We returned late that evening, very weary but happy and thankful for the experience. We then took our flight back to the States. We were so thankful for the privilege of visiting those sacred Biblical sites.

A few years later friends in Fort Collins urged us to lead a tour for them. They got a number to go so that both my wife and I travelled at no charge. This time we flew into Amman, Jordan, and visited sites in Jordan before going across the Allenby Bridge into Israel. We were able to stand on Mt. Nebo and survey the land of Israel as Moses did. We also visited ancient towns on the road down to Petra. We had a good Arab guide who had memorized much of the Pentateuch and would quote verses concerning the sites as we passed them. We rode horses into Petra, a most fascinating place. Then it was on to Israel and all the historic sites.

After Israel we were scheduled to go to Cairo, Egypt. As the tour bus was going south we heard that there was a rebellion in the Egyptian army and the country was under military law. The bus driver decided to keep going and we had to hurry to get to Cairo before dark, when there was a curfew. That was a wild ride; we went blasting through little villages, chickens, donkeys and people scattering before us. When we arrived our driver spread his prayer rug, knelt and thanked Allah for safety! We discovered our hotel had been burned by rebels and they housed us in the Ramses Hotel, a luxury hotel. The accommodations were great but we were kept inside while tanks rumbled up and down the streets. After two days we were able to take a plane back to the States.

Later I was again asked to lead a group and we took the same route as the above except for Egypt.

There were two families from Colorado working in Albania, the Youngs and Dindingers. I was encouraged to visit them for some ministry and decided also to visit Israel and Greece. I left March 6, 2000, for Israel and spent some time with George Kahlil in Nazareth and Bethlehem. J. B. Nicholson was leading a tour and I spent one day with them, enjoying the fellowship with old friends. It was a joy once again to visit ancient sites but also to spend time with the dear Arab Christians there. One day it was hot in Nazareth and I drank some water from Mary's well. That was a mistake; I became deathly sick for several days after I arrived in Greece. I left for Greece on the 15th and spent time with John Kremidas in Athens and Patras. There were opportunities to teach the Word in both areas. John and Irene were friends from years past. Apart from that sick spell in Athens it was a good time.

I left for Albania on the 20th and was met by Ron Young at the airport. I stayed most of the time with Ron and his family in Elbasan but we also traveled around the country to smaller towns and villages having meetings. I also spent some time with Phil Dindinger and his family. Phil has the drive of an evangelist, constantly witnessing. Both families are doing a good work. I also visited George Sturm in Pogradec, where he was planting an assembly. Several assemblies came together for a baptism and it was a joy to have a part in that. Ron also had some contacts in Kosovo and we made a trip up there through Macedonia. The desolation of the war was still evident. It was exciting to see this land which had been so oppressed by Communism, now free and open to the gospel.

It was with real reluctance that I said goodby to the dear saints in Albania and flew to Rome on the 30th. I wanted to spend a few days with the Dan Pasquales before returning home. I had come to know Dan years before when he was in the army and stationed in El Paso. I stayed with them in Nettuno and had some meetings with the assembly. Italy, like much of Europe, is not an easy field for the gospel, but God is working. Dan also showed me the Military Cemetery there where thousands of U. S. soldiers lie buried. Stark white crosses covered acres of dedicated land. It is beautifully landscaped but a sad place as one thinks of all the young men who died in battle in the prime of life. And I was thankful and prayerful that I came out of that conflict alive and could live to serve God. April 3 I returned home.

I had been invited to do Bible teaching in Korea. The first time I stayed with Doug Neiswinder and Ho Sook, his wife. Doug was a missionary from Colorado Springs and had been a friend for some years. The assembly work in Korea had grown rapidly after the Korean war. There were many young Christians hungry for the teaching of the Word. They would tape my messages and then send them around the country. It was an exciting experience to fellowship with various assemblies in Seoul and other places. I ate their food and often slept on a mat on the floor, Korean style. After my first visit there a brother asked me, "Did you eat our food?" When I said that I had he was surprised. "Many Americans won't," he said, "It is too spicy!" They do use lots of red pepper. After being there, when I come home our food tastes very bland. Joon Park translated for me often and did an excellent job. He had lived in the U. S. for some years and spoke English well.

We had worked with many Chinese students from Taiwan who were in graduate school. They urged us to come over for a visit. We had a Chinese Bible class for some years; some were saved and all profited from the teaching. It was a very warm

APPENDIX 2: IN JOURNEYS OFTEN

relationship; they were often in our home and called us "Mom and Dad." The Chinese insisted on paying our air fare and treated us royally in Taiwan. They took us around the island and arranged meetings with former students. Marie counted over thirty of our former students that we visited. It was a delightful time. At times some of them come back to Colorado and visit us.

A few years later they wanted us to return. March 31, 1998, we made another trip to Taiwan and saw certain areas we had not seen on the first trip. It is beautiful, lush, green islands with some high timbered peaks. And again there were meetings with former students, most of them now teaching in universities. We also visited two assemblies but the work is weak in Taiwan. Buddhism is strong with temples everywhere. Marie hurt her leg while traveling and ended up hobbling. I was scheduled to go on to Korea for Bible teaching and she insisted she could get home by herself. The airports do have wheel chairs and we availed ourselves of one to get her safely on the plane going homeward.

Then I went to Korea and Doug picked me up. That Sunday I was at the Kwanak assembly in Seoul, a large, vibrant group of around 250 people. The assemblies there usually eat the Sunday noon meal together, a happy time of fellowship, sitting in their family units on the floor. That evening it was a joy to fellowship with John and Beverly West, who were there for meetings. They had been missionaries in Taiwan years ago, dear friends of ours.

Monday morning Joon Park took me down to a new one-year Bible school that had recently begun near Osan. It was called the Christian Training Institute and was a one-year program. They had scheduled me to teach each morning from 9:00 to 1:00; I took up 1 and 2 Timothy and Titus. The teaching is by interpretation so it takes longer. We had 32 men and women, a mature group. Some were in the Lord's work full time and some were elders. All were hungry for the Word. Laurie Cowell from Australia taught for two hours in the afternoon.

I tried to go for a walk every morning before breakfast to get some exercise. The school was out in the country, a delightful place to walk. I would climb up a hill, through a picturesque farm village with ancient red, tile roofs and then along a road through rice paddies freshly planted. The morning fog gently veiled the surrounding mountains. Beautiful! After a farewell party with gifts I left for Japan and meetings there.

Don Livingston met me at the airport in Osaka on Saturday, April 18. I had not seen Don for more than fifteen years but I quickly recognized him. He is very tall and stands out in a crowd of the shorter Japanese. I had known his parents well, a dear Christian family in Tucson. We had to ride three trains to reach his home in Kurashaki. Donna, his wife, had developed Parkinson's disease but they were determined to stay on in Japan and to serve the Lord. The small assembly met in their home on the ground floor. Sliding screens and doors opened to form a meeting room about 15' x 25'. About forty people attended. "During the B. of B. [Breaking of Bread] I was deeply moved. Here I am at a B. of B. with Japanese. 55 years ago I was in action in the S. Pacific on the Mobile, shooting down Jap. planes and engaged in shore bombardment. I wept much during the B. of B."

Monday was a day of rest with a trip to the inland sea, a beautiful area. Then Tuesday Don and I went to Osaka and stayed in the Budd's house. The Budds had been missionaries there until his tragic death. The house was still used for the radio broadcast that Don was carrying on with the help of a Japanese evangelist. I spoke at Izumi, a vigorous assembly, and later at Higashi Sumigoshi and Sakai City. The meetings were followed by question times; they face some of the same issues and problems that we do. I was deeply impressed by the work in the Osaka area; they are zealous and enthusiastic. I felt a real bond with my brothers and sisters in Korea and Japan.

I left for home on Friday, April 24 and arrived in Denver the same day! One gains a day flying east. It was good to get home and to discover that Marie was feeling much better.

In May 1999 I was back in Korea and although very weary, spoke at the Buku Bu assembly in Seoul after my arrival on Saturday. They asked me to teach on elders and deacons. Then it was teaching at Christian Training Institute. Dear brother Lee

Ok Yong is the principal. This time they asked me to teach the Minor Prophets, a subject I had not taught for some time. After this I taught Timothy and Titus again. It went well and the students again were most responsive. I also spoke at several assemblies in the area. After my two weeks at Christian Training Institute I was again at Kwan Ak assembly for meetings over the weekend of May 23, a very good time with the dear saints. I then went to Inchon for daily meetings and stayed with Kang, Young Kil. He had been a major in the army but resigned to give himself to the Lord's work, a dear brother. I concluded my meetings on May 31 and flew home.

"These three weeks in Korea have been good. I love the Korean people; they are earnest, zealous Christians, hungry for the Word. And they want me to come back."

On Wednesday, May 10, 2000, I left for Seoul again. Sunday I spoke at the assembly in Namsa and then classes began on Monday the 15th. That year the school was in a new building, a lovely structure, with a small apartment for the visiting teacher. I ate with the students and the food was as hot as ever! I took up Timothy and Titus that first week, good interest but fewer students than the last year. I spent the weekend in Inchon with good meetings. Brother Kang is working much with foreign workers who come to Korea to work for two years from various countries in Asia. Sunday evening the assembly serves them a meal. Then the gospel; is preached and translated into the various language groups, a good work. The second week at school I spoke on the Minor Prophets again with good interest. Tae Wan, a Korean who lived with us while he got his PhD., came down from Seoul for a visit.

I left for Osaka, Japan on Saturday, May 27, and stayed with Brother Ogawa, a Japanese worker. There was limited English in the home but we managed to communicate! I was at the Sakai assembly for Sunday. The Breaking of Bread was at 10:00 a.m. and Don said, "Every man will take part." And they did; brother after brother was on his feet worshiping the Lord. It was a great meeting. Then we ate together at 12:30 p.m. and had a teaching meeting at 1:20 p.m. Then at 3:00 p.m. I spoke again, this time in the gospel. They had about thirty men and women coming who were "seekers." They were not saved but were interested and open. They may come for months before making a firm decision. It is a zealous, loving assembly, a hive off from Izumi.

Monday night I was at Takstsuki assembly and Tuesday at Higashi Sumiyoshi assembly. Wednesday I spoke at the Fuse assembly and then Thursday, June 1, I spoke at the Izumi assembly. The next day I left for home but my flight took me to Seoul first and then to Los Angeles and home. It was good to be home, but sad to leave those dear brothers in Japan.

On Tuesday, May 15, 2001, I left for Korea again, arriving in Inchon on the 16th. I spent the rest of the week with brother Kang and the assembly there. The week before had been busy. We had sold our old chapel in Greeley and bought our new building. Then on Monday we moved out of the old building. I had five meetings in Inchon on Friday, Saturday and Sunday. Sunday night was the meeting for foreign workers, with translation into Korean and simultaneously into Chinese, Russian, Mongolian and Pakistani. A number have been saved through those meetings. Then Monday I went to Nansa and began my lessons at Christian Training Institute. It was good to be back; I took up the Minor Prophets the first week and the Tabernacle the second week. The 25th-27th I had meetings in Seoul with Northgate assembly (Buku Bu), a happy time of seeing the saints there again. I left for home on June 1 and had a safe flight, very grateful for my time in Korea once again.

To the Christians in Rome, Paul wrote: *"For I long to see you, that I may impart to you some spiritual gift, so that you may be established—that is, that I may be encouraged together with you by the mutual faith, both of you and me"* (Rom. 1:12-13). Paul was keenly aware that their fellowship would be mutually edifying and encouraging. The Lord's people in various places in the world have greatly blessed my heart and enriched my faith.

Appendix 3

Workers' and Elders' Conferences

In 1933 T. B. Gilbert encouraged some workers in that area to come to his home in Knox, Indiana, for an informal conference. It would be a time of prayer and mutual encouragement. Twelve men came who were interested in pioneer work, in starting new assemblies. They discussed mutual problems and had times of earnest prayer. It was a time of blessing. But that winter Mr. Gilbert's wife developed a deep cough. An exam revealed that she had tuberculosis, a real killer in those days. It was a devastating blow to the Gilberts. Doctors recommended that they move to a warm, dry climate.

In June 1934 they moved to Tucson, Arizon, where they hoped she might get well. But then their only son, Bruce, came down with meningitis and died on March 28, 1937. It was a terrible loss to both of them. The strain of watching him die devastated Mrs. Gilbert. Her health rapidly deteriorated and she died three weeks later, April 17, 1937. It was a fearful blow to Mr. Gilbert. Friends said that his hair turned white overnight. But he kept on in the Lord's work, doing evangelism and having a radio broadcast. He started a small assembly that fall and the next spring visited my mother and me in our humble home. My mother had heard his broadcast and had written him. March 2, 1938, in our living room he explained the gospel to me and I was convicted of my sin and accepted Christ with tears. I am eternally grateful to him for bringing us the gospel.

Because of the illness, T. B. Gilbert had not pursued having another workers' conference for several years, but now his wife was gone. He sent his daughter, Mary Ann, to live with her aunt in Chicago. He was free now to travel and contacted others about having a workers' conference that fall. It was held November 8-10, 1938 in the St. Louis Bible Hall. About 35 preachers came and had a wonderful time. I have a picture of that first conference, some wonderful men of God. I am sure all have gone to their reward by now. It was decided to make this an annual conference. A committee was formed to plan the conferences and brother Gilbert was a vital part of it until he died in 1972. It has continued from that time, except for a few years during World War II when gasoline rationing made travel difficult.

I had visited the conference once while I taught at Emmaus in Chicago, 1950-1952. It was held in Champaign, Illinois, that year. But then I was busy and did not get back for some years. In 1960 Ben Tuininga encouraged me to go with him to San Diego, where the conference was to be held that year. I went, saw the value of it, and was encouraged to work with the conference. Some of us saw the blessing of such a conference, while fiercely refusing to become a legislative body. There was a time when some brethren in Chicago with *Interest* magazine urged us to make decisions as a conference and then to inform assemblies. This we refused to do. The conference was not to be a legislative body; all of us believed that each assembly was autonomous. Elders must lead in their local churches.

And so the work has continued through the years. I was soon asked to become the executive secretary, helping to organize the conference with suggestions from the workers. We also began to urge elders to come. There was a time when numbers fell off and some even suggested discontinuing the conference. But a number of us refused to quit and the work has grown and seen God's blessing. It is especially encouraging for younger workers, often laboring with the beginning of a small assembly. Here they are surrounded by men of God, men of faith, with a wealth of wisdom and experience. There is a camaraderie, a love for one

APPENDIX 3: WORKERS' AND ELDERS' CONFERENCES

another, that is delightful to experience. Various views may be expressed but we insist that there be a spirit of love and mutual esteem, even though we may differ on some matters.

The work continues with a good committee of men from various parts of the country.

Each year it is held in a different city with assemblies in the area cooperating in providing housing and meals for all who come. This working together has proved to be a blessing for the area. Christians get to know preachers and elders from other areas. It is a stimulating time of fellowship, prayer and teaching of God's Word. We have met in various parts of the country but often rotate from the Midwest to the East. Here are the cities where the conferences have been held since 1960:

1960, San Diego, CA
1961, St. Louis, MO (Southside)
1962, Des Moines, IA
1963, Arlington, D.C. (Cherrydale)
1960, San Diego, CA
1961, St. Louis, MO (Southside)
1962, Des Moines, IA
1963, Arlington, D.C. (Cherrydale)
1964, Winston-Salem, N.C.
1965, Baltimore, MD (Loch Hill)
1966, Flint, MI
1967, Cleveland Hts., OH
1968, Minneapolis, MN (Sunnyside)
1969, Fanwood, N J (Woodside)
1970, Houston, TX
1971, Oaklawn, IL
1972, Lexington, MA.
1973, Des Moines, IA
1974, Denver, CO (S.W. Chapel)
1975, St. Louis, MO (Maplewood)
1976, Washington, D.C. (Cherrydale)
1977, Minneapolis, MN (Sunnyside)
1978, Fanwood, NJ (Woodside)
1979, Chicago, IL (Palos Hills)
1981, Des Moines, IA

1982, Cleveland Hts, OH
1983, Lexington, MA
1984, St. Louis, MO (Southside)
1985, Toronto, Ont. (Don Valley Chapel)
1986, Minneapolis, MN (Plymouth)
1987, Berkley, Hts., NJ
1988, Dubuque, IA (Emmaus)
1989, Windsor, Ont. (Oakwood Chapel)
1990, St. Louis, MO (Southside)
1991, Fanwood, NJ (Terril Road)
1992, Minneapolis, MN (Plymouth)
1993, Toronto, Ont. (Markham)
1994, Wichita, KS (S. Emporia)
1995, Kenilworth, NJ
1996, Chicago, IL (Palos Hills)
1997, Buffalo, NY (Blaisdell)
1998, Wichita, KS (Westside)
1999, Waterbury, CT
2000, Lawrence, KS
2001, Morgantown, WV
2002, Waterloo, IA
2003, Baltimore, MD (Forge Road)
2004, Omaha, NE (Keystone Chapel)
2005, Hollywood Bible Chapel, Hollywood, FL
2006, Westside Bible Chapel, Wichita, KS
2007, Terrill Road Bible Chapel, Fanwood, NJ
2008, Lawrence Bible Chapel, Lawrence, KS

Appendix 4

Koinonia house history

In June 1970 the Donald Norbies moved to Greeley from California after much prayer and at the urging of Don and Donna Neilson, our son-in-law and daughter. A small group of college students had met from time to time in homes for several years. In the fall of that year the small assembly began to meet in a large room in our basement at 2605 14th Ave. Court. We had good meetings there and the Lord blessed. Sunday nights Marie made a meal for the group, a good time of fellowship.

In time the group became too large for the basement room. In 1972 a large house at 829 17th Street was purchased by Don and Marie to be used for the assembly. Don Neilson felt it was better that the building not be owned by the assembly. The house had belonged to the Methodist Church and had been used in time past for their campus work. The house was terribly run down and much labor was put into refurbishing it.

The basement was fixed up and rented to men. The assembly used the large living room-dining room area for our meetings. Girls rented the upstairs bedrooms. There was a happy spirit of fellowship. Rental funds paid the mortgage each month.

We named the house Koinonia House from the Greek meaning "fellowship." We also organized as a campus organization in order to use campus facilities for outreach and Bible studies. Dorm Bible studies were productive. A number were being saved and added. We had baptisms nearly every month. Seeley Lake was often used for baptisms and a pool at a health club was used in the winter.

The Belly of the Whale was a garage converted into a coffee house. Steve Chostler lived there and was the genial host. His main problem there was the spiders! Steve hated spiders. The weekends especially were busy times with students coming in.

Intensive Bible studies were conducted regularly. A survey of the Old Testament and New Testament with book studies and doctrinal studies were offered. Some were interested in New Testament Greek and this too was taught. Years later Greg Ebert came back to visit us. He said people often asked him where he went to seminary or Bible school. He tells them he got his training in Greeley!

The assembly continued to grow and to flourish. We sent teams for outreach to Laramie and Rock Springs in June 1975. We also did some outreach in Sterling and Fort Collins. Trip Moore had moved to Quebec City with a burden for the French work. Less than 1% are believers in that needy province. Don Norbie visited him in September 1976 and they looked for an apartment for Don and Donna. They felt called to move there to help the French work.

After Thanksgiving that fall we had a special meeting to bid them goodby. The tears flowed. We had worked together for six years and had seen much blessing. We were different in gift and personality but made a good team.

I wrote about our personal parting: "Then the parting—our hardest yet. Tears flowed and we embraced fervently. Donna clung to me sobbing, Don too—I felt so close to him. It is like an amputation and there is a deep, hollow ache."

Through the winter and spring dissent grew in the assembly, especially over the role of women. Because of my conservative stand I came under attack. In April 1977 the other men in leadership affirmed their support of me. But the attacks continued.

That summer Don and Donna came back for a visit, a happy time. But in the fall on Nov. 6 the strife came to a head and the fellowship divided. Many simply wanted peace and went to other churches. We had 22 couples and 15-20 singles leave the Koinonia House. It was the most distressing time of our service for God.

The work continued on but the back of the assembly was broken. Some had gone off to start another work, but this did not continue. Church trouble leaves a stench in the community. We loved then, and love still, all who were a part of our fellowship.

We bought the house in 1972 and decided to sell it in 1985. The Lord opened up the purchase of a church building at 1203 12th Avenue. For a few years we stopped our Sunday morning meetings and went over to Ft. Collins to help the assembly there which was struggling. But in 1989 we restarted our meetings with six people; two couples we had seen come to the Lord joined with us. In May 2001 we sold that building and bought our present chapel at 2100 22nd Street. This gave us more room and ample parking. Also it is accessible for wheel chairs.

The assembly still functions along the simple lines of the New Testament church, as did Koinonia House. We emphasize teaching of the Word, the Breaking of Bread every Sunday and leadership by elders. We encourage the development of gift. We are still a loving, close group. If you are in Greeley do come and visit us.

My wife and I are now in our 80s. Pray for us that we will finish our course well. For fifty-five years we have served the Lord along simple faith lines. God has been faithful.

On July 24, 2004, a 30th year reunion was organized for the Koinonia House people by Carol Rouch and others who had been saved and helped in those early days. We wondered how many would be able to come from the many students we had contacted during that time. About sixty or seventy came from the north and south, east and west. Thirty years had passed since most of us had seen one another. There were lots of hugs and tears of joy. Memories were exchanged and lives reviewed. Children and families were introduced.

It was a delightful time, a time when some of the wounds caused by the division years ago were healed. After the catered meal there was a lengthy time of singing some of the old hymns and choruses. There was also a time of testimonies with many standing to tell of their conversions and growth while at the University. Then we had the Lord's Supper together and finally reluctantly parted to go to our various homes. We thanked God for being a part of His wonderful family. One day we shall all be together, forever! *"For brethren to dwell together in unity."* (Ps. 133:1)

Epilogue

Well, this writing is finished. It has been lengthy but exciting to review old diaries and to consider the amazing way that God has led us. I have been thankful again for a wife who has been so faithful and sacrificial. We have entertained hundreds, even thousands, in our home over the years. She is an excellent cook and hostess. A man who had been released from jail just left our home after staying for a month. Now he has a job and his own quarters. I believe he wants to live for God.

I began this with a desire to leave an account of our lives for our grandchildren. It may be that some others will be helped. Paul could say toward the end of his life: *"And I thank Christ Jesus our Lord who has enabled me, because he counted me faithful, putting me into the ministry"* (1 Tim. 1:12 NKJV). I grew up in such a humble home. But as a young man in high school I turned to the Lord and gave my life to Him. My only regret is that I have had but one life to give Him and that I have not been a better servant of His. With Paul I can say, *"But God forbid that I should boast except in the cross of our Lord Jesus Christ, by whom the world has been crucified to me, and I to the world"* (Gal. 6:14).

I am more convinced than ever that the simple pathway of faith which the early apostles followed is the best way to serve God. I believe in the pristine pattern of the early church for worship and service. And I believe that God is still able to provide for His servants in wonderful and awesome ways. Elisha asked,

"Where is the Lord God of Elijah?" (2 Kgs. 2:14) as he struck the Jordan and the river parted. He discovered the God of Elijah was also his God.

In 1999 as we were coming home from camp in Minnesota I became sick and had tremendous abdominal pain. Marie drove most of the way home and I went to see our physician. He examined me and sent me to a surgeon. This man sent me immediately to the hospital for surgery. There was a growth on my colon and he said it looked like cancer. That was a miserable night. I was given a strong laxative in preparation for the surgery—but it kept me up all night.

The next morning as I was waiting for surgery the nurse came in. She said, "You are going to have a roommate. Your wife has broken her ankle and is scheduled for surgery also." Marie had slipped on wet grass, fallen on her foot and had a bad break. She managed to drag herself into the house and called a neighbor who took her to the hospital. What a blow! I was counting on her to care for me as I recovered. They brought her in and we both lay there side by side waiting our turn.

There could have been much anxiety but we both commented on the deep sense of peace we had. I have never known a deeper sense of being in the arms of God, surrounded by His love and care. Instead of fear there was a sense of awesome euphoria. All would be well.

I went in first and Marie went in later. When the surgeon came in to see me later he smiled and said, "It was benign, no cancer." But they performed standard cancer surgery, removing half of the colon. And I gradually made a good recovery. Marie had to have a steel plate and thirteen screws inserted to repair her ankle. But she too has made a good recovery. The Lord has been so good.

Doctors are aghast that we have no insurance. When I went into the Lord's work in 1949 preachers were not covered by social security. So we have never had social security nor health insurance. Our doctor and hospital bills that year were over $30,000.00 but as each bill came due we had the funds needed to cover it. We received gifts from people we had never heard from before. One unknown believer sent a check for $3,000.00!

EPILOGUE

The God of Elijah is our God today. We can only praise Him.

As we near the end of our pilgrimage it is our prayer that young men and women who are called of God to serve Him in full time work will get to know the God of Elijah. He is still the God who is able to provide for the needs of those who serve Him. There is no greater honor or work. My wife and I humbly thank God for the privilege of serving Him all these years.

Donald L. Norbie
January 23, 2004

**Life is a Mountain:
God's Faithfulness in the Life of Donald Norbie**
Donald Norbie
B-7934

To Order:
Toll Free: 1 800 952 2382

E-mail: orders@gospelfolio.com

Mail:
GOSPEL FOLIO PRESS
304 Killaly St. West,
Port Colborne ON L3K 6A6

Visit our Webstore where you can shop 24/7
www.gospelfolio.com

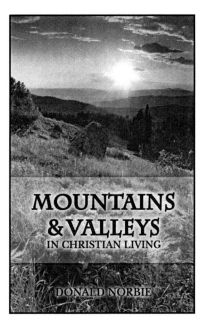

Mountains and Valleys in Christian Living
Donald Norbie
B-17941

   This book covers several important subjects for the believer as illustrated from personal experience or from Bible characters. It deals with: Our Desires as Christians, Security of the Believers, Spiritual Growth, True Riches in Life, Christian Acceptance, A Pattern Life (as found in Joseph), Being Fruitful in Old Age. These topics have been selected by the author as he reflects on his own personal Christian life with it's challenges, trials, and triumphs, work and witness, study and sharing during the different stages of his life.
   The author is sharing these truths with the readers to encourage them to decide to always put the Lord first in their lives. It will not always be easy but we should be motivated to serve the Lord who purchased us with His Own precious blood. He reminds us that our life of service is the only reasonable thing we can give our Master.
   Be encouraged as you take time to read through these short meditations and words of wisdom collected from a life lived by faith in serving his Lord.

Coping with Tragedy
Donald Norbie
L-7159
Booklet: 4" X 6"

    Donald Norbie shares some of his personal experiences. His aim is to encourage each reader to trust the Lord daily throughout life.
    We all appreciate the Lord during the good times of life, but in difficult times we really get to know Him in a special way. The purpose of this booklet is to illustrate to the reader how the Lord provides His grace and strength when needed, especially during our most difficult experiences.
    The Lord knows all the details regarding our experience. He will provide for us according to His will and pleasure.
    Share this booklet with those you know that need a little encouragement during their time of trial and testing.

Toll Free: 1 800 952 2382   E-mail: orders@gospelfolio.com
Visit our Webstore: www.gospelfolio.com
Mail: GOSPEL FOLIO PRESS
304 Killaly St. West, Port Colborne ON L3K 6A6

Other Books by Donald Norbie

Money: Master or Slave
L-MMS
A booklet on what the Bible says about money. Includes a list of all New Testament verses discussing the subject.

Danny: A Life Cut Short
X-6974
A thoughtful & touching biography of Don's beloved son who was caught up in the drug scene.

Be a Man!
X-704
In this book, Mr. Norbie exhorts men to fulfill their responsibilities in the New Testament ideal.

Baptism: The Church's Troubled Water
X-807
This study will help each candidate for baptism understand and thus fulfill in his own life the true meaning of baptism.

1 Timothy Timeless Truths for Today's Church
X-8100
A refreshing commentary on the epistle of First Timothy. This book is both scholarly and heartwarming; it will be useful to Christians desiring a sound commentary.

Toll Free: 1 800 952 2382   E-mail: orders@gospelfolio.com

Visit our Webstore where you can shop 24/7
www.gospelfolio.com

Other Books by Donald Norbie

2 Timothy And Titus
X-8103
A refreshing commentary on the epistles of Second Timothy and Titus. This book is both scholarly and heart-warming.

Acts: The Pattern Church
X-8113
A commentary on the book of Acts.

Lord's Supper: The Church's Love Feast
X-843
This study stresses the importance of this feast as a New Testament church distinctive, and its weekly observance as an expression of our love for the Lord.

New Testament Church Organization
X-848
This book outlines the organization of the apostolic church and why it is necessary to obey this pattern today. Special attention is given to the rise of the clergy/laity system.

This I Believe
ISBN 9781897117873

Order by Mail:
GOSPEL FOLIO PRESS
304 Killaly St. West,
Port Colborne ON L3K 6A6

LaVergne, TN USA
15 July 2010
189685LV00004B/45/P